Hidden Faith Heroes

Dr. Charles A. Crane
2022

Hidden Faith Heroes
is available at special quantity discounts for bulk purchase for sales promotions, premiums, fund-raising, and educational needs.

For details write
Endurance Press, 577 N Cardigan Ave, Star ID 83669.
Visit Endurance Press' website at *www.endurancepress.com*

Hidden Faith Heroes

PUBLISHED BY ENDURANCE PRESS
577 N Cardigan Ave
Star, ID 83669 U.S.A.

All views expressed within are the view of the author and do not necessarily reflect the views of the publisher.

© Dr. Charles A. Crane 2022
All rights reserved. Except for brief excerpts for review purposes, no part of this book may be reproduced or used in any form without prior written permission from the publisher.
ISBN 978-1-7363842-6-8

"Scripture quotations are from the ESV® Bible (The Holy Bible, English Standard Version®), copyright © 2001 by Crossway, a publishing ministry of Good News Publishers. Used by permission. All rights reserved."

L.C.
Printed in the U.S.A.

Contents

Introduction 5
Eleanor Winters 7
Daddy Buckles 9
Elaine Erickson 11
Charles Halstead 13
Al and Kathryn Fisher 15
Winnie Pepiot 17
Bill and Gladys Washburn 19
Doctor Kadish 23
Marrying Sam 25
    Bennie and Reva Bennett
Children can Be influential 29
    The Moxleys
    The Graves
Herb Strubhar 35
Ralph Hafer 37
The Ruths 45
    Ruth Chenoweth
    Ruth Baker
    Ruth and Tom Bender
Mr. and Mrs. George Alsbury 51
Mr. and Mrs. Clyde Kelly 55
Paul Rees 59
    Shakey's Pizza Parlor
    At the Foot of the Cross
Robert Dale Maxwell 65

Chris Roth 71
Jerry Baker 73
Fred Becker 79
Mr. & Mrs. John (Marge) Gordon 83
    The Parsonage
An Unnamed Man 89
All Faith Heroes, Private or Public, Are Gifted
    by the Holy Spirit 93
    A List of Some of the Spiritual Gifts
The Future of Spirit-filled Christians—Heaven 97
    Biblical Descriptions of Heaven
The Future of Those Who Reject Christ—Hell..................... 99
    Biblical Descriptions of Hell
Epilogue—How God Directs Christians' Lives.................... 103

Introduction

One night, while lying in bed praying, it came to mind how many people had been a very important part of the success of the various churches to which we had belonged, who had never received recognition for their contributions to the work of the gospel and the success of the church. Soon the list in my mind had grown quite long. I believe it is time for these hidden faith heroes to receive some recognition for their considerable contributions.

> "So also good works are conspicuous, and even those that are not cannot remain hidden" (I Timothy 5:25).

I might add that at least they shouldn't remain hidden. Too often we have neglected those who work consistently behind the scenes and are not appreciated, but without them the work of Christ would fail.

Want to know who many of these hidden heroes are, go to church an hour or two early for most any church service and notice all of those who come early. They are indispensable to the Lord's work. They prepare communion, open the doors, greet people coming to church, take care of small children, they teach children's classes, are security staff, and operate the sound and other equipment. The list is long.

In most churches the leaders are well known and receive remuneration and frequent commendations or condemnation for their service and their fame sometimes spreads far and wide.

In the same churches there normally are many behind-the-scenes Christians going about their daily lives of service to our Lord and they receive little or no attention. Without these hidden heroes the church would often fail. These unrecognized servants of our Lord make possible the success and survival of the church.

During this prayer time I decided that it would be interesting and helpful that these wonderful behind-the-scenes Christians, who have blessed the churches where I have been a member, or where I have served as their preacher, receive some long overdue recognition. Most churches have many behind-the-scenes Hidden Faith Heroes.

Eleanor Winters

Possibly the most important person who impacted my whole life for Christ was a neighbor lady named Eleanor Winters.

The Winters family, Shorty and Eleanor, moved in next door to us when I was in the third grade in school. They became friends with my parents and Dad and Mom led them to Christ. Our families became lifelong friends.

The Winters had no children of their own, but both of them loved children and welcomed them into their home. They lived in a large, old sort of a mansion of a house, next door to us. It had a porch that ran across the front and down one side. It was two stories high, with a garage complex in the back yard.

Shorty and Eleanor helped raise Eleanor's sister's children. Their family name was Gosser and since their mother had suffered a bad case of polio after having five children, she was in a wheelchair and not able to give good care to her five boys. The boys' dad spent his time at the pool hall half or completely drunk. These young men were often with the Winters. There was Melvin, Bob, Dwight, John, and Denny.

The Winters also welcomed Shorty's brother's two boys, who came often, but not as frequently as the Gossers. I remember Donny Winters who was sort of a rascal. He got me into trouble several times, as I was along when he did some stupid thing like knocking on people's doors at night and then running.

Another of Shorty's nieces was named Diane and the Winters raised her from early grade school until she was married. I remember playing with this pretty, freckle-nosed, girl next door. I was a few years older than her.

Eleanor's love of children led to her soon teaching our Sunday morning and evening Bible classes at church. She led us in Bible drills, seeing who could find passages quickest in our Bibles.

She was strong on memorization and we learned the books of the Bible by heart so we could name all 66 books in order. She had us memorize all of the scriptures on a chart called "The Church Revealed in the Scriptures." There were about 350 verses on this chart.

Eleanor, a bit later, began to teach a release time Christian education class at her house, which was near the grade school. I attended these classes in her home once a week. We were let out of public school during a school day to attend these classes.

Being sort of a frisky kid, one day when Eleanor had to leave the room, I sneaked up and got under her desk. When she returned she planted a well-placed kick to my ribs. I let out a yelp and she exclaimed, "Oh Chuck, what are you doing under my desk!" She was on to me as soon as she had returned to the classroom and saw that I was not in my chair.

From the beginning to the end of her teaching there was no doubt that she loved us kids and only wanted what was best for us. There were many other good teachers who blessed us children, but Eleanor taught me more about the Bible and faith than any other person, including my own parents and our preachers.

Eleanor was a hidden hero of the faith. She impacted so many children for all of their lives. It is a challenge for each Christian to offer their talents to care for children, to work in Sunday school and build faith in children. Want to be a Faith Hero? Help with Sunday school or child care.

Daddy Buckles

As a youth minister at a small church, while attending Bible college, I was expected to preach often on Sunday evenings. These sermons were, at best, of questionable quality of preaching. At that time I hadn't even taken a class on homiletics (preaching).

In the church was an old man, with white grey hair, stooped shoulders, dressed in clothes that were clean, but old and worn. He would sort of look up at a person as his head was bent forward by arthritis and he sort of had to look out sideways, with bright blue eyes. His face would light up with a smile and then in a rather tired and coarse voice he would speak.

Not one time did I ever hear an unkind or discouraging word from "Daddy Buckles." Each time I preached, after finishing I would think, "That sure didn't pan out like I had hoped it would."

Daddy Buckles would shuffle up to me, sort of look at me sideways from his bright blue eyes and say, "That was about as fine a sermon as I have ever heard from such a young preacher." It wasn't a lie, but it was his way of encouraging a young preacher. "About as fine" were his kind and warm words.

Of course, there were others who offered criticism and were quick to point out my deficiencies. These left me rather sad and sometimes discouraged. Still today I observe those members who spread around their own deficiencies by picking on the preachers.

As I look back, it was not the critics, but Daddy Buckles, who has had a positive part in my ministry ever since. I think of him with a heart of gratitude because he encouraged and reinforced my humble beginning efforts at preaching and provided the motivation for me to try harder to become a useful preacher. Thanks, Daddy Buckles, you were a Hidden Faith Hero.

For the rest of you, save your criticism of the preachers for your periods of prayer for him and the other servants of the church and Lord.

Elaine Erickson

In our very first ministry, in a small town and church, one of the key reasons for the stability and success of the gospel was due to the behind-the-scenes efforts of Elaine Erickson and several others like her. Elaine was in her mid-thirties or maybe very early forties. (I've never felt comfortable asking a lady's age or weight.) She was beautiful in a feminine sort of way. She was petite, always well dressed, had dark, almost black, hair, dark brown eyes, and a ready smile for everyone. Most everyone who knew her loved her.

Elaine was a beautician in the small town, in fact, the only one. If a lady wanted her hair fixed Elaine was her only choice. As the preacher, I soon learned from several ladies who showed up at church, that Elaine had spoken to them of her faith and had invited them to church.

Elaine soon discovered that my wife and I were terribly poor and that my wife could not afford to have her hair fixed professionally. In a subtle and kind way she asked my wife if she would like a permanent. She replied that she would, but could not afford such luxuries. Elaine said there would be no cost. This turned into a weekly visit to the beauty parlor for Margaret as Elaine made her hair look beautiful for Sunday services where she was in front of the congregation at the piano or organ.

After a few months the small village was hit by what was called "The Columbus Day Storm." The city experienced all sorts of destruction. The most serious damage at the church, was to the church building's roof. The roofing over my desk had blown off and when I came to my office Friday morning to continue work on my Sunday sermon, I found my only Bible had been right where the worst leak was. The Bible was totally soaked and had swelled to being three times as big as it had been before.

It was the Bible that I had used through Bible college and it was filled with notes and references. The ink, from my written notes, had faded and blurred and it was almost unreadable in many places. It was a total mess. I was in a tearful panic, but I could not afford a new one, not even a cheap one. My other old Bibles had been discarded due to moving, lack of space, and being worn out.

That Sunday, imagine my embarrassment when I tried to preach using it. It was still wet and all out of shape and three times the size of what it had been. It still was shot. We sometimes did not even have enough money for food, let alone for me to spend $50–60 on a new Bible. I tearfully prayed that Sunday night, asking God what to do.

The roof was repaired immediately. On the next Tuesday morning when I went to the office to do my church work, there next to my old ruined Bible was a brand new one, the same translation, but much nicer than the old one had been.

There was no indication just where it had come from, but with a bit of sleuthing around, it was learned that Elaine and her husband, Floyd, had purchased it and left it on my desk.

Without a doubt, dear Elaine was one of the most valuable members of the church, but she in fact was a hidden faith hero. A book could be written about all the ways Elaine served the Lord at the church, yet she never taught a class nor sang a solo. But she served the Lord every day. The church would not have been the same without her.

When it was time to move on to our next ministry, she came and tearfully expressed her sorrow at our leaving. Her parting words were, "When we get to Heaven I will be waiting near the Eastern Gate looking for you so we can renew our friendship in Heaven." We'll be seeing you Elaine—you were and are a beautiful Hidden Faith Hero.

Charles Halstead

I've written before about our trips to the river for baptisms, often at night with car lights shining on where we would be baptizing people. One night, one of the ladies had a call of nature at the baptism and going out in the bushes in the dark, she fell off of a high bank and broke her leg. This led us to realize that we needed a baptistery in the church building.

I had gotten busy and built a baptistery in the front of the church, just behind the stage wall with an opening so it could be seen. It took weeks and it was not classy, but it was strong. It remains in use now 58 years later. Soon after completion, one of the men from the church came and wanted to talk to me about being the first to be baptized in it.

I asked him about his previous baptism and he confirmed that he had been baptized some twelve years earlier. He explained that in college he had met this beautiful lady who was now his wife; her name was Carolyn. He had grown deeply in love with her but Carolyn insisted that she would not marry him unless he was a Christian, and so he had been baptized. He humbly confessed that he was baptized into Carolyn, not Christ, as he really did not believe in Christ as Savior and Lord, but was willing to be baptized if the reward was marrying Carolyn.

He had been really faithful in attending church to please the wife whom he loved so much. He had slowly grown in faith until now he wanted to truly commit his life to Christ and be baptized. We arranged for his baptism the following day and he, Carolyn, and I met and he made the good confession and was immersed as the very first one to be baptized in the new baptistery.

Out of this baptismal experience, we became close friends with many hours of sweet Christian fellowship--hunting, fishing, being together as families and in the work of the church. Chuck was a teacher at the high school and also football coach. This gave him considerable influence for Christ in the small community. He now made no secret of his faith, inviting people to church and speaking of his faith in classes at school and in the community.

He was a very great coach of the football team and even though the school was small they ended up that same year winning the State championship for B level schools in Oregon. I believe I attended every home game that season. One of our fine young Christian men, Alan Cherry, was a star player on the team. I stood at the goal line when Alan carried the winning touchdown in the championship game that year. Alan was tackled just six inches over the goal line.

One of the things that led to this championship was Chuck's teaching the players to sort of hide the ball they were carrying so no one knew for sure just who had it. The many different hand-offs they used to disguise what they were doing confused the other teams.

On several occasions I was standing on the goal line when the winning touchdown was made.

Chuck became a member of the deacon board and was a wise and willing worker and always encouraged me in the work of ministry. He was often a source of wise counsel behind the scenes.

His beautiful wife, Carolyn, was a registered nurse and gave good health advice to the members of the church. Their three children grew up to be a credit to their family and the church. The Halsteads served behind the scenes but were a strong part of filling the church to capacity with warm and loving members. They were "Hidden Faith Heroes." Both have now gone on to their heavenly rewards.

Al and Kathryn Fisher

During the first few months of our ministry in this small town, the Fishers became members of the church. Kathryn was the head nurse at a hospital in Roseburg, some thirteen miles away. She was tall, her hair was beginning to grey, and she was somewhat athletic. I saw her as rather austere but kind. She was a fine Christian woman.

Her husband, Al, was a logger, also a dedicated Christian. He had a special job in the woods. He was a "high climber." When a logging site was set up, they needed a "spar pole." This was at the site where logs would be yarded in so they could be loaded on log trucks and hauled out of the woods to the sawmills. One of Al's jobs was to prepare the spar poles.

This meant he would take a chain saw and climb up a huge fir tree at the proper place, in the center of the logging site, cutting off the limbs as he climbed. When he came to the top of the tree he would top it and then attach the cables and pulleys. Then the tree would be stabilized with several cables attached near the top of the tree and at the bottom to stumps or trees nearby, and a long cable was run through a big pulley and fastened clear across the place being logged and fastened to what was called the "donkey." This powerful diesel machine was on skids so it could be moved around as needed.

They would attach chokers to the long cable to pull the huge logs back to the landing near the spar pole. This was called the "haul back" cable and it ran from the pulley at the top of the spar pole to a stump or tree across the long distance where trees had been felled and back to haul in the logs. Al was known throughout the area as a master at setting up spar poles.

When Margaret was pregnant with son Steve and beginning to show, Kathryn asked to talk with me at the church door as soon as people cleared out from the morning church service. I was puzzled as to what she could want.

When she spoke she said, "Pastor Crane, as a preacher, you will never make much money. You cannot afford to have a large family as you will never be able to support them. If you will come over to the hospital I will explain to you what causes babies so your family will grow no larger." (You can imagine my embarrassment, but she was a matter-of-fact person and probably thought I didn't know what caused those babies. After all I was a preacher.) In reality I was raised on a farm and did know what caused babies.

But that was only the beginning of the story of the Fishers. Al was a first-rate gardener and always had a huge garden, which might have been called a "truck garden." When the garden began to produce, we were blessed with all sorts of things: carrots, beans, tomatoes, radishes, and especially corn on the cob.

Our phone would ring in the early evening and Al would ask for Margaret. He would say, "Are you fixing dinner? If so, put on a pot of water to boil because I have just picked the corn and I am bringing you a bag full." A few minutes later, here came the load of fresh vegetables. We were so poor this food sometimes made the difference between us going hungry or eating a balanced diet with nice fresh vegetables.

The Fishers were so encouraging and loving. Later I suggested to Kathryn that I had been raised on a farm and knew what caused babies. My heart is warmed by thinking of these Hidden Faith Heroes. I'm looking forward to seeing them again before long. They have long ago gone to their eternal rewards.

Winnie Pepiot

An older single lady moved to town. She came to town for several reasons. She had two sons with families that lived there. One was Leonard and the other Rodney. Both families were members of the church. Leonard owned a gas and oil distributorship and Rodney was a successful logger.

Rodney had a disabled daughter, Vickie. The night of her graduation from high school, Vickie was in a bad car wreck and was left a paraplegic. She was confined to bed or a wheelchair for the rest of her life. Winnie wanted to be near to help Vickie and to enjoy her family and grandchildren. She became a regular member of the church and was always in the church services.

Winnie was the consummate example of a good "grandmother." She liked to cook and bake cookies. She dressed like a grandmother should. She was warm and loving. She always wore her hair in sort of a bun on the back and top of her head. It was not long before she became a favorite with our family and children.

My work schedule was enormous. I was teaching Sunday school and preaching Sunday morning, teaching youth meetings and preaching Sunday evenings. Wednesday evenings I was leading prayer meeting and teaching a class. I was trying to make at least 25 calls on members or prospective members each week. I mowed the church and parsonage lawns, and painted the church building and the parsonage, which had not been painted for years.

Winnie soon saw the picture and knew Margaret needed help with the children. She volunteered to sit with our children any time we needed someone. She in reality became their grandmother too. She would come to our house for an afternoon or evening, or for a day or two. We could leave the children with her at her house or ours. She didn't expect much warning but cheerfully would tend the children at a moment's notice. She was so loving and kind. She would never accept any pay.

Frequently we would take her with us for a ride to Crater Lake on Sunday after morning church and make it back in time for Sunday evening assembly. We would take a picnic lunch and eat it looking out over this spectacular lake and then rush back home.

It became my practice to visit her granddaughter Vickie every Monday afternoon. Vickie became a close and dear friend. The Pepiots and Leatherwoods, especially Winnie, were such behind-the-scenes Faith Heroes.

Bill and Gladys Washburn

A few blocks west of the church, was a street that ran south from Main Street. It was called Ash. A couple of blocks down the street there was a sort of shack surrounded with weeds and garbage.

The house was small, probably a kitchen, small living area, bedroom and bath, maybe eight hundred square feet. Alongside the house was a carport with an old, run-down wreck of a car in it. Everything spoke of neglect and deferred maintenance.

The neighborhood kids told me they went and picked up the beer bottles and beer cans from the yard, sold them to get the 35 cents needed to go to the mid-day show at the theater. The beer containers had been thrown by Bill into the tall grass and weeds along with all sorts of other garbage.

The small town of Sutherlin was not a high-class place, but this was definitely the most disgusting yard in the community.

I was concerned and learned that the person who lived there was named Bill and he was probably one of the most notorious, living, town drunks. At one time he had been somewhat successful as an entertainer, having some good musical skills that he used to entertain in bars, night clubs, and dives. During those years he had sampled the goods too often until he was overcome with alcoholism.

Bill had come near the end of any usefulness he had ever had and was facing death from booze and neglect. His neighbors detested him, and his wife. Gladys. was also separated from him. He was an outcast and useless to God and man.

One of the members invited Bill to church and he showed up one Sunday night. As was my custom, I visited him in his little shack that same week. He was reluctant to let me in, but by being warm and friendly I finally was permitted to enter his pigsty of a place.

We talked about his life and learned the history of his decline from being a useful and talented musician to his present miserable state. He looked and smelled awful. He had a big beer belly, ugly beard, shaggy hair and no sign of what he had once been before his decline into total dependence on alcohol.

He had reached the end of his life and all he had left was despair. We talked about Jesus and redemption found only in Him. I took him through the book of Romans on what has been called "the Roman Road to Salvation." In a few weeks he was baptized and he gradually began the climb out of a disgusting life of failure.

Not too many weeks later Bill asked if it would be all right to bring some of his musical instruments to church on Sunday evening and play along with the piano and church organ. He began to do this with his guitar, then mandolin and banjo.

People loved his creative approach to music and he would also provide some solo performances which were loved.

He asked if he could invite a few other members to join him at evening church service, with their instruments and add to our evening music. He did and slowly it grew into a small band. Bill and Margaret worked together, with him directing the little orchestra, and it became common to have a nice instrumental performance at evening church that people enjoyed. Soon people began to come to hear the music and I then had the chance to preach the gospel to them.

He who had been the town bum was now drawing people to Christ and the church and salvation. Not long after this, his wife returned to him and then they renewed their vows of marriage and the little shack on Ash Street began to look cared for and the grass and weeds were cut down. Gladys cleaned the house, Bill got his hair cut and beard trimmed, and slimmed down, as he was now back on a healthy diet. But most of all, Bill became a Hidden Faith Hero, using his fine talent for music to praise the Lord and draw people to Christ.

The only complaint I heard was from the kids who lost their movie matinee money because there were no more beer cans and bottles.

The lesson I learned was that no one alive is beyond the redemption that comes in Christ our Lord. Never give up on anyone as long as they are alive, Christ loves them, and we should also. When a person becomes a Christian God will clean them up and they can use their God given talents to serve Him and lead people to Salvation.

Bill Washburn became a true Faith Hero.

Doctor Kadish

This is not the doctor's real name as I do not want to embarrass him, as he did prove to help me and other local ministers without charge.

As a child of two years of age I drank gasoline and aspirated it into my lungs and for two months lay near death before finally recovering.

An uncle, who lived next door, had left a small can of gas sitting near the back door of our house. It had a spout and round cap on top and a little wire handle with a wood handle to hold on to. It was bright red and the cap on the little spout had been left off. I picked it up and tried to drink from the can as I must have been thirsty. When the gasoline hit my throat and stomach it was blown into my lungs and sinuses. I was found strangling and was rushed to the doctors. For two whole months my mother, Jessie, rocked me and cared for me. Most of the time, for those two months, she said that I was near death.

Finally I recovered but the result had been frequent respiratory infections and frequent pneumonia. When I got very tired or did too much speaking I would end up sick.

So, being sick, Kathryn Fisher suggested that I see Doctor Kadish. I went to his office with pneumonia, rasping, and breathing with difficulty. I recall the waiting room where there were green leather chairs with chrome arm rests. On the wall was a long light that was purple. It was supposed to kill germs.

I was placed in a room and soon the doctor came in. He said to me, "So you are the new preacher at Your Neighborhood

Church." I replied, "Yes, and I'm sick today." To this he said, "I'll try to help you but may not do you much good as I had a devil of a time getting through medical school. I still wonder why they graduated me, so maybe together we can figure out what is wrong with you and get you well."

My confidence level was near zero, but he sent me to the drug store in Roseburg to get some medicine to take. In a few days I was better.

I soon learned that Doctor Kadish's main skill was knocking holes in your confidence in him as a doctor. One lady that I had been asked to take to him was laying on her back on the examination table, fully clothed and he was humming and puzzling as to what was wrong with her. He finally went into his office and came back with a medical book that he opened, laying it on her stomach and paging through it. Finally he said, "Guess I don't know what is wrong with her, you need to take her to the hospital in Roseburg."

We did, and she had a broken leg and soon had it set with a cast and in a few weeks was recovered.

Anyway, Doctor Kadish never charged me or our family anything for helping us and usually we knew our problem before going to see him and he would prescribe a proper medicine.

He wasn't a Hidden Hero, but did help us when we had no money to pay, so does qualify as a hero in our time of need. He did have special skill in killing any confidence one had in him as a doctor.

Marrying Sam
Reva & Bennie Bennett

Not long after beginning the new ministry in Southern Oregon, a middle-aged couple showed up at the morning church services and became members. They seemed substantial, clean, intelligent, and Christian. I immediately liked them and felt we would be friends, which we were.

The lady was named Reva and her husband's name was Bennie. Their last name was Bennett. They had two grown daughters and one still at home who was a senior in high school.

I visited them in their home and Reva explained that she was a teacher at the high school and Bennie explained that he was a foreman at the local plywood mill. It didn't take long for Bennie to explain that he liked cars and not to be surprised if he had a new car every year.

They settled into regular attendance and soon became involved in the church, having been Christians for many years. They became a supportive and happy addition to the church family.

Before long Reva invited me back to their home as she had something she wanted to talk to me about. Upon arrival she explained she taught in the sociology department at the high school and wished to have my help in teaching a couple of lessons each semester on marriage. This was to be in two different classes, (juniors and seniors) that she taught at the school. She wanted me to come twice to each of these classes.

In a few weeks I was standing before two classes taught by Mrs. Bennett. The subject was to be about marriage and I was to teach two hours to each of the classes on two different days.

I separated the lessons into two sections, the first on dating and working toward marriage and a second about the marriage ceremony and keys to a happy married life.

In the first class I talked about four things: 1. Friendship, 2. Courtship, 3. Engagement, 4. and Marriage.

In the second class I discussed positive ways to make a happy marriage and the four major pitfalls that cause marriages to fail. In retrospect these classes were not masterpieces of wisdom, but did offer help that would have otherwise been non-existent.

The result was that when these senior students graduated and later wanted to get married they came to me to perform their ceremonies. I was soon getting scheduled with more weddings than I could handle. I remember one day when I had three weddings in one day, one home and two church weddings.

I was informed by the person granting wedding licenses in the County Court House that I had more weddings than any other person in Douglas County. This provided a wonderful opportunity to turn these young families to Christ and the church.

Reva, although she never was very obvious at church, had a strong witness for Christ in a unique way at her job of teaching high school, she was a Hidden Hero.

This led to many happy, unusual, and strange events. I remember the day when the bride fainted during the vows. I had to get a chair for her to sit on for the rest of the ceremony.

Then there was the wedding where the ring bearer decided he didn't want to give me the rings. You can imagine the scene with the best man chasing the little kid, while he ran and yelled all over the sanctuary trying to get the rings. Yes he did catch the little fellow and the ceremony continued.

Another time when I asked the father of the bride, "Who gives this woman to be married to this man?" The father replied in a nice clear voice, "I do her husband." Wow, did he get razzed at the reception. One friend said to him, "Yes I would like to get rid of my wife, but wouldn't do it in front of the whole church and at my daughter's wedding."

The end result of Reva's hidden testimony was that the whole community ended up in our church building for weddings and me even having the weddings for the daughter of the high school principal and other city officials. This was why the church grew from a few people to having the building packed for each church service and many people giving their lives to Christ and being baptized.

And yes, Bennie did give me rides in his new cars each year. I remember one new car, it was a Ford Mercury. It had a big motor and was a beauty. The Bennetts were Hidden Faith Heroes, and that's how I picked up the nickname, "Marrying Sam."

Children Can Be Influential

I'm not sure this story should be told, but you will have to be the judge.

As a child of 13 years of age our Sunday school teacher, Guy Womack, made us read the Book of Revelation if we wanted to go with him on a campout to Clear Lake. We had to read the whole book, which I did.

As I got to chapter 6:12–17 which says:

"When he opened the sixth seal, I looked, and behold, there was a great earthquake, and the sun became black as sackcloth, the full moon became like blood, and as a tree sheds its winter fruit when shaken by a gale …Then the kings of the earth and the great ones and the generals and the rich and the powerful, and everyone, slave and free, hid themselves in the caves and among the rocks of the mountains, calling to the mountains and rocks 'Fall on us and hide us from the face of him who is seated on the throne, and from the wrath of the Lamb, for the great day of their wrath has come, and who can stand.'"

This made a great impression on me.

A few days after reading this, in our area, we had a bad forest fire and the sun was turned black during the day and at night the full moon was red from smoke.

About two weeks later there was a huge shower of stars that happens about once in seventy years. I saw all of this and just knew I needed to get right with the Lord because He was about to come in judgment of me for the miserable things I had done in my brief life. I had not committed great sins, but things an overactive 10–13 year old and a few naughty friends did to "have fun."

At the same time we were having our annual revival meeting with Archie Word, as evangelist. I remember he dressed like he had just come out of a fine men's store, shoes polished until you could see your reflection in them. His white shirts and nice suits were perfection. But most of all his preaching was powerful. On Friday evening when the invitation hymn was sung I was the first down the aisle to accept Christ.

It was the beginning of everyone responding to the invitation, except for the elders and preacher. Second down the aisle was my brother David.

That was December 13, 1951, which was, to the best of my memory, the coldest day I could recall. The church building did not have central heat, but a big wood stove. The baptistery was not full since it would have frozen during the cold days. We waited while it was filled. The water was ice cold.

This was justice as at age seven, in mid-July, I was sitting with two buddies, Roy and Edwin Ledford, in church and it was awfully hot. Edwin leaned over and said, "Let's go get baptized, it would be just like going swimming and cool us down, it is terribly hot in here." The next thing we knew we were being baptized (swimming?) in cool water. Later I felt a terrible guilt about this foolishness. It was only justice that the water for my real baptism was ice cold.

When Dave and I were baptized we were about frozen. The preacher had fishing boots on with wool socks and his wool suit. We were in our Levis. He had me in the water, prayed, expounded, and finally baptized me. I am not sure why I was shaking so hard, was it a chill, or was it the Holy Spirit? Whatever it was, there was no doubt I had experienced a new birth. My life has been changed ever since.

Homer Moxley

It was just three months later that I was out squirrel hunting on the back of our ranch when I saw a big Caterpillar tractor yarding a huge peeler log down the road. My thought was someone was stealing our timber, so I stood in the middle of the road with my rifle on my hip so the man had to stop.

The tractor stopped and the most handsome man I had ever seen got off and came to me, taking off his glove he shook my hand, saying "I am Homer Moxley and your father has given me permission to yard my logs across the back of your ranch."

Homer Moxley immediately impacted me. He was so handsome, with curly hair that was sandy colored, with a tint of blonde and red and waves. His Caterpillar tractor looked brand new. He was dressed in clothes that looked like he was ready for church. He spoke with a charming southern drawl. I later learned he was from Tennessee. Somehow we bonded that day and this bond lasted the rest of his life. I had his funeral when he was 94. The day we met I was 13 and he was 34.

It was one of the few times in my life when I bonded immediately with another person. It was mutual. We were friends from then on. A few weeks later he came to visit me and said he wanted to give me a gift of the Book of Mormon. He explained that he was a Latter-day Saint or Mormon. He said if I would read this book, after prayer, God would give me a burning in my bosom that it was true. He asked that I promise to read it prayerfully, which I did, beginning that very night as I went to bed.

For the next many days at bedtime I got on my knees and prayed and then read it. Fortunately, Eleanor Winters, at church, had taught me the Bible and also God did guide me. I would read, then I would run down stairs to check out things I was reading in the Book of Mormon with our World Book Encyclopedia.

I still have this Book of Mormon with my notes from when I was but a child. I was filled with questions due to the many clear errors in the book. I came away with a "burning in my brain" that this was a book of garbage.

In a few weeks I asked Homer if he would help me with my study of the Mormon book. He agreed. When he tried to explain my questions, they became his questions also. In a few weeks he accepted the real Jesus and was baptized as Acts 2:38 instructed. Homer became a strong and influential Christian with national influence for Christ.

His logging operation grew into a contracting business that prospered beyond imagination. At one time he had 27 contracting jobs going for the United States Army Corp of Engineers. A bit later he became a member of the Board of a Christian university with worldwide influence.

He was featured in a national Christian publication for a prayer event in his life as a contractor. He was doing a job for the Army in which he was moving the whole side of a mountain, just above a massive new dam in the river.

He was running behind on this job, and the man from the government who had hired him came to Homer and said they were projecting that he would be several weeks late completing the job and they would have to fine him $100,000 a day for each day he was late. They said they would not fine him if he would have his crew work seven days a week and around the clock, three shifts a day.

Homer replied that he would not make his crew work on the Lord's Day since he and many of them were Christians. He said he would work extra shifts but not make his crew work 24 hours a day, as that would endanger their lives. He asked the boss if he was a believer and if he believed in prayer? To this the man replied, no he was an agnostic and did not believe the tripe about answered prayer.

Homer said, well I do believe in prayer, so let's pray and ask for God's help right now. The man laughed at Homer, but Homer raised both hands above his head and asked God to help him complete the project on time.

As Homer prayed and when his huge earth moving machines were at both ends of the job, the whole side of the mountain began to slide down right to where they were hauling it. In about 20 minutes the whole mountain had moved and Homer told me they finished the job two weeks earlier than planned. This story ended up with pictures in a national Christian magazine. Homer said to me, "God does still move mountains when we pray."

When Homer was an old man, I visited him in a nursing home in Salem, Oregon. He was in his wheelchair going around the home praying for old and sick people and teaching them about the Lord and salvation. He was a minister of Christ until his dying day. This was due to a 13-year-old kid who let the Lord use him. Yes, children can have a huge influence for Christ and need to be encouraged to do so. They can be Hidden Faith Heroes.

The Graves

At age 15, I met and was impressed with a vivacious and beautiful blonde little gal named Sally. We never had a date since she was only 13 and I just 15. Her father, George Graves, said he would let her attend our Sunday school some if I would agree to study the Book of Mormon with him.

(It was years later that I learned that my home town was a Mormon settlement; this explained all these LDS people there.)

Sally did attend Sunday school and church some with me, but we never had a date or even ate a hamburger or drank a milkshake together, except sometime later having lunch together in the school cafeteria. We rode to and from church with my folks.

A few weeks later I honored my promise to her father George and brought my book of Mormon for him to teach me. We and his three children, Goldie, Sally, and Butch, sat round the kitchen table. I opened my Book of Mormon and asked him to explain the passages that had bothered me. (His wife had died a few months before.)

George tried to explain these and finally said, "Well, I have read it but guess I never did read it carefully as I was assured by my church it was true. Let me research your questions and then we can meet again."

When we met again George confessed that he was convinced that the Book of Mormon was a yarn, not founded on facts and he no longer believed it to be Scripture. He said he wanted to get a fresh view of Jesus and salvation.

George, a widower, and his three children, were soon baptized into the real Jesus Christ. He became active in the church and began to preach the gospel. This he did for years with considerable success. As he aged, one Sunday during his sermon he had a heart attack and died.

Thankfully George had found the salvation promised in John 3:16:

> "For God so loved the world that He gave His only Son that whosoever believes in Him should not perish but have eternal life."

In the meantime, George and his son Butch have both gone on to glory.

I look forward to the time when we can sit around the banquet table in heaven and talk about studying the farce called "The Book of Mormon" at their kitchen table.

Children can have profound influence for Christ. We need to teach them how useful they can be to the kingdom. They certainly can be Hidden Faith Heroes.

Herb Strubhar

Another young person who was a blessing to the church was my dearest friend in grade and high school, his name was Herb. The story has its beginning when I was a third grader.

Next door to us moved in an older family, Shorty and Eleanor Winters (already mentioned) who had no children of their own but often had other family members' children. They had Diane, Shorty's niece, come and live with them for several years. She was two years younger than me.

Diane was fair skinned, with blondish hair and lots of freckles. She and I became friends and often played games together and were in church together for Sunday school, Daily Vacation Bible School, and church. We remained friends all of our lives. She has since passed on.

In the fourth grade a new family became Christians and members of the church, the Strubhars. They had four children, one of which was Herb. He was a fine young man, but mischievous. He and I immediately became friends and chummed around and graduated from high school together.

When I decided to become a preacher, Herb and another friend, Marvin Cline, both wanted to become loggers. They promised that when I was trying to live on a preacher's skimpy wages they would send me money to help me.

Unfortunately, both were killed in logging-related accidents. Herb got hit by a speeding freight train in his log truck and was killed instantly. He was 24 years old. Marvin was setting up his small travel trailer in the woods, with his wife and daughter inside, when the jack slipped and the trailer came down and mashed his head like cracking a nut, killing him instantly.

The purpose of this story is to tell you how Herb was a Hidden Hero. Herb married Diane Winters, who had been our neighbor when I was in grade school. They proceeded to have four children. Herb and Diane loved people, especially poor people. Herb and Diane would buy lots of groceries and deliver them to some widow or divorced lady with children.

The week before Herb was killed they had taken a widow lady with four children to town and bought all of them new shoes. He left a big hole in the church when he died, as he was full of good works, helping the poor, sick, and families whose fathers were in jail.

The New Testament is quite clear when Jesus says, "I was hungry and you fed me, naked and you clothed me, in jail and you visited me." He explained that if you helped the less fortunate it was like helping Him. This is a good work for a Spirit-filled Christian, not one for public glory, but with bountiful rewards in Heaven. Dear friend Herb, you were a Hidden Hero, may others follow your good example.

We look forward to seeing you again soon, Herb, over in Paradise.

Ralph Hafer

Ralph has been the subject in other books I've written, but he deserves additional coverage here as he was a great Hidden Faith Hero.

God has His way of putting people where He wants them. Even though our time in the small southern Oregon town had been filled with wonderful people, we were called to our second ministry in Salt Lake City, Utah. It was not my idea to leave Sutherlin, Oregon. Looking back, God had prepared me for years for the next great adventure of ministry.

God had been preparing me for this new responsibility since I was a boy 13 years old, when I first read the Book of Mormon. Just three months after accepting Christ and being baptized, I helped lead the first Mormon to Jesus. A short time later, a second LDS family came to know the real Jesus. These are the stories just told.

I traveled by Greyhound bus to Salt Lake City, to be interviewed for the pulpit of a new church plant. It was the first independent Christian Church in the State of Utah. The church was young and not yet able to survive on its own. It was more of an idea than a reality yet.

After preaching and being interviewed by several church men, I was strongly considering accepting their offer of becoming their preacher.

After church that morning an "old man" came up to me and said, "Young man, if you accept the pulpit I will become a member of the congregation and do what I can to support your ministry." I had no idea who or what he was, just an old man. I did not know he was one of the great Hidden Faith Heroes.

Ralph Hafer

When we had settled into the new ministry, one of the very first to become members were Ralph and Margaret, this old man and his wife. Someone then asked if I knew who they were. I had no idea but the person said that Ralph was a very rich businessman. That was a great understatement, as I would learn before long.

Ralph and Margaret sort of adopted me as a son along with Ralph's other son and three daughters. His four children were each married and had their own very busy lives. About that time my father, Claude, died and Ralph became sort of a stepfather to me.

He loved the church and its work and requested to go with me, whenever I needed to travel in ministry, especially when traveling out of town or state. We traveled weeks and months together, thousands of miles, over the next seven plus years. He told me about his life from the time he was a small boy.

When he was nine years old, his mother and father both died of typhoid fever from bad water on an Iowa farm where they share cropped and lived in a small shack where the drinking water came from a cistern that was filled with water from the roof of the house. Both of his parents became ill from this bad water and died. Ralph's only living relative was his 14-year-old brother. Ralph told me they had no known relatives or family anywhere.

The boys had no place to go so decided to catch a ride west on a nearby railroad train. They put their few possessions in a couple of gunny sacks and boarded the next train west.

Two days later, Ralph's older brother got into a scuffle with a hobo who was also heading west on the same train. The hobo pushed Ralph's brother off the moving train, which ran over him and cut him into two pieces. Ralph told me he had to go to a nearby farm and borrow a shovel to bury his brother's broken body. He was now truly alone at nine years of age. His schooling had ended for good in Iowa where he had been in the middle of the third grade.

Having no other choice, he caught the next train heading west with the two sacks of things. He ended up working as a "roust-a-bout" for Buffalo Bill Cody, where he did what he could to help the wild-west show for his food to eat and a place to live.

At age nineteen he learned he could homestead a piece of land at Gooding, Idaho. He told me he was so poor that on his new farm he planted his first garden, using a wood roofing shingle to work up a small garden near an irrigation canal. He didn't even have a hoe or shovel. He said he pulled up the sagebrush with his bare hands. Thus began his farming venture.

Along the way he had picked up a few bad habits, one of which was smoking, but not drinking. He worked hard on his homestead and gradually built a modest house. He said that from the time he first got the farm he had always loved junk.

When he had a few hours of spare time from farming he began buying pieces of broken machinery, tractors, farm equipment, broken trucks, and pickups. No one else wanted this junk so he paid very little for the things he bought.

He told me that he sold the good parts off of this broken equipment and when everything useful was gone he sold the rest for scrap metal. He lived off of what he earned farming and began to invest much of what his "junk hobby" had produced.

He eventually married Mina and ended up with three daughters and a son, George. He said that there was a revival at the local Christian church where he and his family sometimes attended. He was about fifty years old when he accepted Christ at the revival and was baptized.

He said the next day he was standing in front of the fireplace in their house when he became convicted he needed to stop smoking. He placed his pack of Camels on the mantel of the fireplace and said, "Lord, deliver me from this filthy habit." He told me he never smoked another cigarette. One year later he saw the cigarettes still lying there and he threw the package of Camels into the fire.

A few months later he decided he wanted to pursue his love of junk but could do so much better in a larger city so decided to sell out and move to Salt Lake City, Utah. He sold his place and his field of junk and they moved to Utah.

He said he was convicted that he had never tithed his income so he gave half of the money he got from the sale of his farm in Idaho to the only Christian church in Salt Lake. It was a Disciples of Christ Christian church near downtown.

He took the rest of his money and bought twenty acres of land on Second West and Second South streets. It was just a field of weeds.

In Salt Lake City he again began collecting junk and selling parts. Two months later the state highway was re-routed in front of his property, making it one of the prime places for business in the whole valley. He credited this stroke of good fortune to God blessing him for catching up on his tithe.

He ended up not only buying and selling parts and junk, but before long became the dealer for one major new truck line. By the time I knew Ralph he had ninety men manning the phones and shipping truck and auto parts all over America. His business became the largest such independent parts business west of the Mississippi River.

In the meantime he became interested in the penny Salt Lake stock market and took some of his spare funds from junking and with almost magical skill invested in millions of dollars of stock, bonds, and penny stocks.

But whenever a person would meet him and was with him, he was a humble and gentle, old, Christian man who always quietly bore his testimony of his Lord Jesus.

Boyd Packer, son of the prophet and president of the LDS church, worked for Ralph and he introduced him to me and through study and prayer was baptized into the real Jesus. Boyd Packer's grandson is now the preacher of the Christian church we once served. He earned his ministry degrees from a major Christian church seminary.

Ralph and I traveled many places together. I was on the Board of the Navajo Christian Mission near Four Corners, Arizona, for six years. He always wanted to go to these meetings with me and often did. He became a member of this Board along with me.

I also served as a member of the Board of Directors of Intermountain Bible College for years. When possible he went there with me. I also served on the Intermountain Church Planters Board and he liked to go to these meetings.

When I would go to speak at men's meetings or at churches, we traveled together. These were times of great learning for me.

Although he had very limited education, ending his schooling half way through the third grade, yet he was possessor of a brilliant mind. Some of his words of wisdom I recall are, "It takes wind to fly a kite." After hearing him say this many times, one day I asked what this meant.

He explained that to run a business, a church, or even a college, one must advertise. He asked, "Did you ever try to fly a kite without wind?" He explained that one could run their legs off and as soon as they quit running the kite would flutter to the ground. He explained that his business did so well because he advertised in all of the surrounding states. He told me that advertising was the wind that made a business fly, like wind causes a kite to fly.

He said on another day, "Work is too hard to do to not have money working for you." I asked for him to explain and he taught me about investing. He said all people have limited energy to work. When tired the work stops. Investments keep on working when you stop.

He explained that most families used up all their salaries just to exist, eat, pay the bills and tithe, often wasting the rest. If they had investments, these investments would continue to work day and night 365 days a year. He especially stressed to not waste time, or money, on useless things, but to find something that you enjoyed doing to divert your attention from your normal work load and that could earn extra income for investment.

He said that was where his junk hobby had blessed him and his family. Instead of fishing, hunting, playing golf, or watching lots of TV, he had fun with his junk. This was how he had prospered financially. He said once you have some investments they begin to earn and increase. He explained that the term "stock market" was taken from the idea of buying calves and raising them to sell for profit. Stock, cows, and livestock grow without you having to do much work on them.

In his business he had realized that people would work harder if each employee had a stake in the business. He was one of the first to introduce profit sharing with his employees. When the business did well, so did the employees. Many of his employees eventually became multi-millionaires.

Salt Lake had a penny stock market. Shares of stock were sometimes just a few cents each. One day he came to me and gave me an envelope with some penny stocks.

There were 11,000 shares of Modern Mineral stock. It was valued at 11 cents a share. It rose to be valued as high as $1.27 a share. I was out of town and when I got home it had declined to 97 cents. I thought I would keep it until it was over a dollar again and then sell it. Sometime later I sold it for 11 cents. I learned another lesson: don't get greedy, take your profit and move on.

But gradually I learned investing from him, and one penny stock made me $3,000 in three months when he said it was time to sell it.

Another insight he taught me was the importance of location for a business or a church. He said the three most important things in planting a church were location, location, and location. He said the same was true in business.

He stressed how important hard work and learning how to treat people with dignity and respect were to success in whatever work one does. He was such a gentle, wise, and kind man.

Another day he said if you are going to discuss a large business deal, take the person who you are to discuss business with, to a nice lunch. You buy, eat lightly, and encourage the other person to eat well.

Then wait a half hour and when the person's blood has traveled to their stomach to digest the food you will be sharp and they won't be. Then you can work out a good deal. He said, "Never cheat anyone" but it helps to be sharp when doing business, so you don't get cheated. Don't be the one with a brain starved for blood when doing business.

He told me one day that since his conversion he and never belonged to a church where he was not the number one giver of money. He said he was careful to not give so much that others did not have to do their part. He said when he gave he wanted it not to be known. So often the Hafers were the difference in the church prospering or failing, but few knew. They were Hidden Heroes.

These are just a few of the ideas Ralph taught me. One day he said his Chrysler car motor was misfiring on one cylinder. He had it tuned up twice and it still ran poorly.

I asked to borrow it for a day and took it home and found that it had one bad spark plug, the last one at the right rear of the engine. It was impossible to take it out without taking loose the motor mounts and raising the engine a few inches. I did this and with a new spark plug the car ran fine. The mechanics didn't expend the energy to really fix the car. He never forgot this repair to his car.

Another day I was at their house and his wife, Margaret, had all her clothes hanging outside to dry. I asked why she didn't use her clothes dryer. She said it hadn't worked for months. I asked why she hadn't had it fixed and she said they were conserving their money so they could give more to missions and the church.

I had my small box of tools in the car, got them, and found that one electric wire to the dryer had a loose nut and it was not making contact. It took me 15 minutes to fix it. When I got in my car there was an envelope on the front seat with two $100 bills in it.

Years later I received a phone call from Ralph. He asked if I would have his funeral. I asked if he was ill. He said no but liked to have his business in order. I agreed and a few days later, when I was supposed to pay on a note at the bank, for money I had borrowed to give to the church's new property fund, here came a check for $750 as a retainer for doing his funeral. I did this funeral several years later. This money I took to the bank the day it came and paid on the borrowed money for the new property. The money was due that day.

Some years later his wife, Margaret, was ill and not expected to live long. I went to see her in SLC. After visiting with her I laid hands on her and prayed for her. I then asked if she would give me a "matriarchal blessing" so she asked me to kneel in front of her and she laid her trembling, old, feeble, hands on my head and prayed a marvelous prayer, concluding by saying, "Never worry Charles, when you can pray, Amen."

The Hafers never preached, taught, sang solos, nor did much to be seen, but I doubt anyone had more influence for the Lord and good of the church in Salt Lake City than they did as they were Hidden Faith Heroes.

The Ruths

Three fine ladies named Ruth qualify as Hidden Faith Heroes. The first was Ruth Chenoweth. She came to America just at the close of World War II with an officer whose wife and he had adopted her since her parents were both killed in the war and she was orphaned.

Ruth Chenoweth

She was naturally beautiful, petite, dark haired, beautiful physically and with a cute accent since her native tongue was German. It was easy to love Ruth and when she and her husband, Leo, became members they were immediately loved by the whole church. They had two adopted children, Mark and Michelle.

Ruth did not teach a class, sing in the choir, did not have any public position, but her presence was evident. She had a gift of making things beautiful, when she was around things began to look classy.

She made a cover for the Communion Table that was deep purple with a gold tasseled fringe around it. She put up discrete decorations in both the men's and woman's bathrooms that made them inviting. On special days beautiful flowers would show up, Easter lilies on Easter and on special days. We soon

Ruth Chenoweth, right

knew that the church building's warm and homey atmosphere could be traced to dear Ruth.

She was Leo's second wife and I learned that his first wife had died at 24 of breast cancer.

One day I got a tearful call from Leo and out of his awful grief finally got it out of him that Ruth had died that morning. She was suffering with the flu and went to the doctor and he had given her a shot, which by mistake, was wrong and it had killed her.

I will never forget being with Leo at the grave yard picking out a place for her burial and his anguished cries to God asking, "Why will you never let me be happy?"

We took Michelle and Mark into our home for months until Leo was able to provide care for them again in his own home.

But looking back, a part of the success of the church during that time was the wise and beautiful things Ruth did around the church building to make it warm and inviting. It was just better than most any other church building because Ruth was there, a Hidden Faith Hero.

Ruth Baker

One day I was leaving my church office and just about into my car in the parking lot when a big, black, Lincoln Continental pulled up next to me, and a pretty lady put down the power window. The lady introduced herself as Ruth Baker. She had her left hand on the steering wheel and on it was a huge diamond ring, maybe four carats.

Ruth asked, "Will you baptize me?" I was sort of taken aback and replied, "I'm not used to having people drive into the church parking lot and ask to be baptized. Will you come into my office so we can talk about this?"

She had been studying Acts and Romans and had learned that her being sprinkled, in place of immersion, was not what the Bible taught. She said her Methodist preacher insisted sprinkling was good enough and he had no way to really baptize her anyway.

That evening she brought her husband, Jim, and she was baptized. They began to attend church regularly and she volunteered to be my secretary, insisting she had good skills, which she did.

Ruth began to work for me and did she have skills! She could type faster than the electric typewriter could keep up. She could take shorthand faster than I could talk. She soon knew every member of the church better than I did, with information about what was happening in their lives. She proved super valuable.

There was one problem. She was a big lady. Her husband told me that when they married she was thought to be the most beautiful woman in the county. Then she soon after began to add weight.

Don't misunderstand me, being heavy does not mean being ugly. She was still a massive beauty, just full sized. I've seen many large and beautiful women. She was the classic example, but this did not mean there were no issues.

In the second week of her employment, mid-morning I heard a massive crash in her office and heard her cry out. Going to check, I found her in the midst of the pieces of her broken secretary chair. She hadn't been hurt but the chair was a total loss.

The next day I shopped and found a heavy-duty model which I bought. It lasted about two more weeks. We finally settled on metal folding chairs that were guaranteed for life. These chairs sort of worked until she twisted without getting up and they would crunch down.

When I took a trunk load of them to be replaced, I was questioned about what we were doing to these chairs, since no one else had ever ruined even one of them.

What is the message to all of this? Ruth went on to glory years ago, but while working at the church she was a jewel of efficiency, soul winning, and information. When they moved, she left behind so much that she had done so well and it was no longer being accomplished. She didn't get much public recognition but was a great Hidden Faith Hero behind the scenes. Thanks Ruth, we still miss you.

Ruth and Tom Bender

One of the first families that we became acquainted with in the Salt Lake City church was the Benders. She was a third Ruth hero. One week to the day after we had moved into the parsonage it burned and was ruined. We stayed three days with another family, the Carpenters, until we found more permanent housing with the Benders.

The elders: Clyde Benton, Charles Crane, Tom Bender, Ralph Hafer, and Fred Getman. Ward Armstrong was out of town when this picture was taken.

Their home had just three bedrooms with a basement. There were four of them and five of us, so we were packed into the approximately 1,900-square-foot house. People were sleeping everywhere. We lived with them for three-and-one-half months. We became fast friends.

Soon we learned what super special people they were. The church parking lot had been turned into a swamp and was not useable. Free donated fill dirt had proved to be like quicksand. Tom and I hauled many dump truck loads of gravel along planks to dump in the muck until it could be used. We loaded our wheelbarrows and hauled gravel evening after evening. We worked and sweated copiously, but soon the parking lot was firm enough to drive and park on.

The next job awaiting us was laying the floor tile in the recently-built church sanctuary. It was just plywood flooring when we began. About the second evening as we worked we noted that we both had blisters on our knees from crawling around on the floor, but we finally got the floor tile laid.

Now it was time to begin serious discipleship, and Tom and I spent many evenings teaching people in their homes. As we spent hundreds of hours together we came to love each other like brothers. During these initial difficult days of getting the church established, Tom Bender was a key to the success.

Ruth did not help us haul gravel or lay tile but soon displayed extraordinary skills in reading people. I've never observed anyone like her. If she had 15 minutes to talk with someone, she could very accurately analyze who and what they were. Her skill was uncanny. She would caution and warn me about people and not once was she wrong. This saved me many possibly hurtful and embarrassing situations. I have no doubt it was a spiritual gift.

These two generous, hospitable, and godly people were Hidden Faith Heroes in this mission church in Utah. The four or five good similar churches planted in Utah were possible because of their wise, generous, and behind-the-scenes work and contribution to the ministry of the church.

Both died young, Tom of a massive heart attack and Ruth of cancer. I always wondered if God needed someone special in Paradise for some hard and important job, so He called them both pretty early. Bless you, dear saints. We look forward to seeing you soon in Glory.

Every church leader needs a few steady members and friends, who encourage and support them behind the scenes. Far too many criticize and discourage the preachers and elders but not the Benders. They were Hidden Faith Heroes.

Mr. & Mrs. George Alsbury

The weekend that I interviewed to become the minister of the church in Salt Lake City, I met George and Lorene Alsbury. They were a mature couple. Tom Bender explained to me that George had just recently accepted Christ and been baptized.

The rest of the 42 members were people from other places whose work had transferred them to Utah, and not being LDS they wanted to be members of a Christian church. The church so far had no other conversion other than George Alsbury since its beginning was just shortly before. Lorene was already a Christian.

I traveled back to Oregon on the Greyhound bus and received a call a few days later from Robert Thomas, who tearfully told me that George had been diagnosed with a very vicious form of lung cancer, probably caused by years of chain smoking and alcohol. I was saddened to hear this and promised to pray daily for George.

Upon our arrival in Utah, George immediately volunteered to enter into a discipleship relationship with me if I would teach him about the Gospel. He and I spent the next few months every Tuesday evening studying and calling together.

Our evening went like this: we would pray together when we got in the car and then as we drove to the homes of prospective members, I would cover some aspect of the Bible or Christian teaching as we drove. During these times George began to tell me about his life. He had worked for years as a butcher for a large grocery store chain.

He explained that over time two bad habits had almost killed him. As a rebellious teenager he had started smoking. Finally he was chain smoking whenever he could, one cigarette after another.

He began social drinking with buddies and at social occasions. After a couple of years he had become an alcoholic, drinking a fifth of liquor every day for almost ten years. He said he went around just barely sober and able to survive on his jobs.

He had not been feeling well and his doctor told him both cigarettes and alcohol had to go. He tried but could not stop, and decided that maybe Jesus would help him quit if he gave his life to Him. He said after his baptism he never smoked another cigarette or had another drink of alcohol.

Our evenings together proved beneficial, and George learned quickly and eagerly. We pretty much covered the whole Bible and teachings about the church. We always began and ended our evenings together in prayer. Several families were won to Christ and a number of LDS came to know the real Jesus through our united efforts.

One Tuesday evening George brought bad news. His doctor had told him on Monday that he had one lung full of cancer and it was beyond treatment. The doctor told him he had but a few more months to live. Our Tuesdays became more intense and we talked about eternity and heaven. George was totally committed to Christ and secure in his salvation.

Soon he was in and out of the hospital, unable to work and mostly convalesced at home. He was no longer able to go with me Tuesday evenings, so I would stop and pray with him at home. He continued to be in church as he could.

On Palm Sunday morning of the same year, my phone rang at 1:30 A.M. and it was the hospital asking that I come to be with George as he could not live but a short time. I arrived at the hospital at about 2:15 A.M. George was in a coma and unresponsive.

I laid my hands on him and began to pray. He sat up, opened his eyes and said, "I'm so glad to see you, Charles." We talked for about 5–10 minutes and the conversation went somewhat like this.

George said, "I was just getting ready to pass over to Paradise and could feel the excitement of being with Jesus, my parents and friends. Is there anyone over there you want me to take a message to?"

I replied, "Yes, George, my best boyhood friend was Herb Strubhar. He was killed in a truck/train accident when he was 24 years old. Would you tell him how much I miss him and that I will remain faithful and be seeing him soon."

After expressing our love for each other, George gave a big sigh, laid back down and after a couple of deep breaths stopped breathing and died with a smile on his face. It was a most difficult time for me as a young preacher.

With tears a few hours later I told about George's death at 2:30 that Palm Sunday morning. I had not been back to bed as I was dealing with the grief of losing this special friend, yet rejoicing in his sure salvation.

What did the Alsburys offer the church? He was the first baptism in the new church building's baptistery. He came from a wasted life and was like a bright light of faith shining to all of us. His role of discipleship with me helped several families come to Christ. One Sunday there were eleven baptisms.

Lorene was rather quiet and demure, but sort of glowed with warmth and she blessed us all with her faith, during George's conversion, illness, and short life thereafter.

George put me in contact with his nephew who was a preacher in Smithfield, Missouri and he and I worked together in three revival meetings where many people came to Christ.

The Alsburys were Hidden Faith Heroes at Southeast Christian Church in Salt Lake City, Utah. The Palm Sunday when I announced his death the whole church was in tears, some were tears of sorrow, but all tears were of joy having known and been blessed by brother George and his sweet wife Lorene, the Hidden Faith Heroes.

Mr. and Mrs. Clyde (Hazel) Kelly

The following events are told as best I recall them from so many years ago. The main points are clear in my mind, but some details may be a bit out of focus.

Clyde and Hazel came to Southeast Christian Church after the church had begun to experience remarkable growth. We were in need of help, but due to several circumstances we could not pay for what we really needed.

The church had outgrown its original sanctuary and classrooms. We were expanding the whole building, the basement and the worship center above. The original sanctuary would seat about 300 and we were expanding it to seat 600 and adding more classrooms in the basement below. Giving had grown remarkably, but so had the cost of essentially doubling the size of the church facility.

Clyde called me one day and expressed his desire to come help with the work of the church in Utah. We visited and I learned that he was a devoted Christian.

He had retired after serving 20 years in the military. He had enrolled in a small college called Dakota Bible College and had taken a couple of years of classes. He had not earned a degree, nor been ordained to the ministry. He said he and Hazel wanted to go to the mission field but lacked the necessary training or funding to meet the requirements to do so. They thought of Salt Lake City was sort of a stateside mission field and it was.

After conferring with the elders, the Kellys were interviewed and hired part time to assist for a few months, six as I recall. They arrived a few weeks later and here is what I recall about them. They proved so helpful that they stayed longer.

Both Clyde and Hazel were trim, clean, warm, industrious, and truly godly. Whatever needed to be done they were ready. Hazel helped in fixing communion, washing the cups, helping clean the building, and working in Sunday school and DVBS. She was hardworking and wonderful to work with. Clyde would mow the lawn, clean up the parking lots, call on the sick, teach the lost and in general he saw what needed to be done and did it without even being asked. They both were treasures, yet Clyde was inexperienced in several areas of ministry.

Clyde was a zealous soul winner, visiting church guests, calling constantly, teaching people the gospel, and it was not long before he came with a middle aged woman to be baptized. She was huge as I recall. Not only was she tall but heavy.

As already mentioned, the church building was under construction. The whole front of the church had been torn out including the baptistery. That end of the Sanctuary was covered by huge tarps to cover the hole and the work in progress beyond.

Since we were the only Christian church for miles around and there were no other places to baptize people, our contractor had brought in a large tank and placed it at the left side and front of the sanctuary. We had to fill it with water with a hose and heat the water with a plug-in heater. This tank was difficult to keep clean, since to empty it we had to siphon the water out and to fill it, we had to wait while the hose filled up the 800–900 gallons of water again.

On the Sunday evening Clyde was to perform his very first baptism, the tank was a little green on the floor and sides. (One boy asked if this scum on the tank was people's sins.) That Sunday evening when Clyde and the lady were finally in the tank after having climbed over the side with a step ladder outside and inside, Clyde said the proper things.

But when he went to baptize her they both slipped and together went under with a mighty splash, and a wall of water shot over the end of the tank onto the sanctuary floor. Both were baptized and when they came up they both were sputtering, choking, and spitting. The congregation did not know just how to respond, so we all clapped loudly; some were stifling laughs.

Well, brother Kelly was off to a good start in ministry, but the most interesting days were yet to come. I'm

Southeast Christian Church

not sure he had ever had a class on homiletics (preaching) but his heart was full of the love of Jesus.

I asked him to give his first sermon on a Sunday evening. By this time the Kellys were really loved by all of us. His sermon was such that I still recall it to this day. I can't remember what I preached during that same period of time, but do remember his sermons. God does often use people's honest and earnest efforts.

Clyde's first sermon was from Acts 17:22–33. His major points were taken from the text and were proper. What made his sermon so memorable was his pronunciation of the word Areopagus. Instead of saying Areopagus he pronounced it "Aero-pay-cuss". My mind turned to Pecos Bill and some wild west stories. Well, his sermon still survives in my mind and my sermons are mostly forgotten.

His next sermon was even a little more memorable. Clyde chose Jeremiah 36:20–26. In this text Jehoiakim, the King, has Jeremiah's prophecies read and he cuts them off piece by piece and burns them. In the King James Version, which Clyde used, it says he read and threw them in the "brazier" or fire pot, or fireplace. In the sermon several times Clyde calls this the "brassiere," with us chuckling and thinking of ladies' clothing, instead of a fireplace.

Soon thereafter we began another church across town and the Kellys went to help with this venture. They never found much fame in ministry, but they were truly heroes of the faith in Utah. The work was so blessed because of Hazel and Clyde Kelly, the Hidden Faith Heroes.

Paul Rees

One Sunday morning a very distinguished looking couple came into church. I greeted them warmly and noticed that they seemed quite special and out of the ordinary. They said their names were Paul and Lucile Rees.

Paul was about 5 foot 10, portly, balding, grey hair, steel grey eyes, dressed in what may have been a Hart Schaffner Marx suit, white shirt, great necktie, and gorgeous cowboy boots and about a four carat diamond ring on his left little finger. Everything matched but the boots. Lucile was also dressed in a beautiful dress, hair perfect, trim, and beautiful. As she spoke I suspected she had Southern heritage.

At that time the church was growing, but still small enough that I noticed a rather significant increase in our monthly income with their addition. I suspected that the Reeses may have been the cause. They did prove to be very generous people.

A few weeks later I came down with pneumonia and was convalescing at home. I received a phone call from Paul and he asked if I had recovered enough that I might enjoy a ride around the area. It was a warm sunny day. I was feeling some better and thought getting out of the house might be beneficial, and I did want to get to know Paul better.

He showed up at our house in a brand new Sedan Deville, yellow and white Cadillac. He said it was brand new and he had just gotten it the day before. He had learned that I liked nice cars and thought a ride might lift my spirits. Our first stop was at the local Arctic Circle for milk shakes, they were large and above the rim. They really hit the spot with both of us.

Paul explained to me that he sold cowboy boots for a living and his area was Idaho, Nevada, Utah, Wyoming, and Montana. He told me his company was the largest boot maker in the world and he did quite well, specializing in cowboy boots, although they had other kinds of boots also. We had a great time riding in his new, top-of-the-line car. From that day on we had a special connection.

A few months later he asked to have a whole afternoon with me. We had lunch together and then went to one of the leading men's stores in Salt Lake. He said I always dressed nicely, but knew that with three small children and a preacher's salary, I might be able to use some new clothes.

He said I was to buy a new suit, shirt, ties, and shoes. He wanted even my under things to be new, including socks. He purchased me the finest clothes I had ever owned.

A few weeks later he brought me the finest cowboy boots I had ever seen, they were Dan Post, handmade boots. I have only worn them on very special occasions and still have them. They were very beautiful, expensive, and still gorgeous.

Paul and Lucile were Hidden Faith Heroes, blessing the church and many families by their grace and generosity.

Shakey's Pizza Parlor

About the same time, another new family became members of the church, Claude and Geraldine Killian. They had three children, a daughter and twin sons. Claude managed the local Shakey's Pizza parlor, and Geraldine worked for him.

We began to patronize them since they had a lunch special they called, "Bunch of Lunch," for $1.99 a person where one could eat their fill of pizza, salad, chicken, and drink. In a short time our small church staff began to meet there almost weekly for staff meetings and to discuss church work.

One of the other regular patrons was a person Geraldine called "Little Jake." I noticed him driving into the parking lot the same time as we did one day. He had a Buick Roadmaster car that sat lower in the left front. When little Jake got out I saw why it sat low. Jake was huge, tall, and enormously fat. He must have weighed 400–500 pounds.

When he began to eat I was flabbergasted. He would put a whole chicken leg in his mouth, sort of twist it back and forth a few times and chew a couple of times and then swallow it all in a couple of gulps, washed down with copious amounts of soda.

What added to our amazement was Geraldine would stand near where he was eating and here is what she said so all could hear. "Little Jake you have eaten two giant pizzas, large amounts of salad and 21 pieces of chicken. You have drunk four giant drinks and you are still eating!"

I got Geraldine aside and asked, "Aren't you afraid you will run him off as a customer?" She said, "That is what I am trying to do. The days he eats here, our buffet loses money."

This gave me fresh insight into Geraldine. She was not afraid to speak her mind, in fact she was always sort of a motor mouth. Somehow the filter between her brain and tongue was missing.

A few weeks later, in the church lobby, with people standing all around, she addressed me in a loud voice. "Charles you do know that a preacher says everything people want to learn from him in just two years! How long have you been here, five-and-a-half years, right? Don't you think it is time for you to move on?"

This prompted me to want to learn more about the Killians, which I did. Geraldine was led to Christ by her husband, Claude. She was Jewish by birth and upbringing, bright, opinionated, and vocal. One person suggested that her tongue was loose at both ends, with a hinge in the middle. She would control most conversations. Now back to Paul Rees.

Claude and Geraldine won a free trip to Southern California by doing so well in managing Shakeys. They were to have a full two weeks on the coast with all expenses paid.

At the time Geraldine was playing the piano and Margaret the organ on Sundays. When the Killians returned from California

Geraldine had no teeth. She had been trying to body surf in the waves and lost her dentures. Frankly she looked pretty pathetic. She didn't seem embarrassed playing the piano toothless.

After church when everyone was standing in the lobby, Paul Rees said to her, "Geraldine, what happened to your teeth?" She told him and he said in a nice clear voice, "Geraldine, it was about time the Lord defanged you! Maybe you will learn not to talk all the time and boss people around."

A few weeks later, the Killians' twin boys came home from college. They were handsome fellows and were great singers. They used background tapes for musical accompaniment. The only thing that was strange about them on this trip home was they had grown their hair long and it was down around their shoulders.

In the lobby after church, with everyone standing around, Paul addressed them. "Hey fellows, where did you come up with those 'heshee' hair styles?" They replied, "What do you mean, Paul?" He replied, "I can't tell if you are a he or a she, so will just call you 'heshees' until you get a haircut." Everyone had a good laugh and a few days later they had nice haircuts.

At the Foot of the Cross

The next chapter in the Rees's lives unfolded a couple of months later. Our neighbor, Larry Siegland, a few houses up the street, came and asked to talk with me. The subject was about Paul Rees. Larry sold men's suits and explained that each year clothiers had an annual meeting in which they discussed how to improve their businesses' effectiveness.

He said, as usual, they honored one of their members who was the most extremely successful. He said this year it was Paul Rees who was honored. It was announced that he was the top salesman for the world's largest boot manufacturer. Paul had that honor and when his success had been told he was asked to explain his success.

Here is what Larry told me Paul got up and said, "I'm so successful because I am so handsome, have such beautiful hair, have such a buff body, am so gifted in gab, I drive a new yellow Cadillac, and am just luckier that many others." After explaining his work ethic and sales method he said to them, "I want to level with you, any success I may have ever had comes from one source. I have submitted my life to Jesus Christ at the foot of His cross. Without Him I would be nothing, and any of you should want to know and work with Him. Everything I do would end in failure without Him."

Larry said to me, "Charles, what does it mean to submit oneself to Jesus at the foot of the cross?" This gave me a wonderful chance to tell him about salvation in Jesus Christ.

Having Paul and Lucile around the church meant there was a generous and wise family who constantly bore testimony to their faith in Jesus Christ. The whole church was blessed, even though he was not an elder, they did not sing, preach, teach, or get much public praise. The church was so blessed by these Hidden Faith Heroes.

Robert Dale Maxwell

Early in my ministry I learned that in the Great Commission Jesus had told us to "Go therefore and make disciples of all nations" (Matthew 28:19). I had checked the word "disciple" to learn its full meaning and learned that a *mathetes* (the Greek word for disciple), meant a "doing learner." I learned that church leadership needed to teach and involve people in ministry.

From further study I learned that an Old Testament *telmed* (the Hebrew word for disciple), meant a learner. There was a vast difference between the Old and New Testament words for disciples. The Old Testament disciple was to learn the five books of Moses. While in the New Testament the disciple was to learn while doing. What were these disciples to be doing? Jesus said; "Go into all of the world and preach the gospel."

For this reason it became my plan to involve people in ministry while teaching them. We began by involving 75 or more people in the local church in ministry and they were to then involve others. This led to significant growth in each of these churches. There were soon actually hundreds involved. Some were extraordinarily effective. One of these was Bob Maxwell.

Margaret did not accompany me at the beginning of the ministry to Eugene, Oregon, as she needed major surgery and could not join me until she had recovered. I was living in my pickup/camper on the church property. One of the families began to hang around the church until most everyone else had left and then to take me to dinner each Sunday after church.

Into this practice a few weeks, Bob asked if I would tutor him in ministry so he could become more effective. I was already doing this with another man, Ken Hodney, so on two nights each week I was discipling these men, while at the same time organizing seventy-five others to involve them in doing church work.

I met each Thursday evening with Bob and we began by prayer and then visited prospective members or prospective Christians. As we drove, I taught Bob about some aspect of ministry. Then we spent time with people in their homes teaching them about Christ and the church.

One family we taught was Darrell and Betty Phillips. They had come to church the previous Sunday. We soon learned that Darrell had been the most successful car salesman in Oregon history, selling an average of 200 cars a month for a year. These sales included large sales to businesses like rental car companies and the state police.

That was the good news. The bad news was that his success had led to drinking and smoking until he became useless as a drunkard and was fired and now unemployed. His doctor had told him he would be dead in two to three years if he did not quit drinking and smoking. Thus they showed up at church.

We taught them, and Darrell was baptized a few days later. Betty, his wife, had already become a Christian and was living faithfully. Bob had a significant part in this conversion as he was head of the automotive department at the local junior college. He and Darrell hit it off due to their mutual interest in cars and Bob began to disciple him.

After about 16 months, one day my executive assistant, Adel Hodney, said to me, "Did you know you are discipling one of America's greatest war heroes?" I replied to her, "You must be kidding me. He hasn't said a word about this."

So that week when Bob and I met, I asked him about this. Bob said, "Oh that was nothing, I was just doing my duty." I asked what awards he received and he humbly said, "Two purple hearts, two bronze stars, two silver stars and the Congressional Medal of Honor." He said, "I was just acting as my Christian faith had motivated me."

It took months to get much more out of Bob, but finally I got most of the information.

In the Second World War he had been in the African Campaign under General George Patton. His job was to travel ahead of the troops and string telephone wire for communication. To do this he carried a 75-pound pack of materials and went ahead of the troops into no-man's land and danger. Sometimes he was two miles ahead of the troops. He had walked from Lybia all the way to Cairo, Egypt, carrying his 75-pound pack.

The next assignment was to take part in the Italian campaign. He entered ahead of the troops in the invasion of Sicily and Italy, walking with his heavy pack the full length of Italy and over the Alps. He said one day he was strafed by an Allied fighter plane and saved himself by standing sideways behind a large power pole, with bullets going on each side of him.

Another day he was with his commanding officer when they heard the sound of an incoming Howitzer shell coming at them. He threw himself on top of his officer and received severe wounds all up his legs and back. His officer was not hurt. He had to be flown to England for medical care and recovery.

When he recovered, he was put back into the war in the Invasion of France that by that time had been overrun by the German army. He was still going ahead of the troops still a mile or two ahead of the Allies. The area they were in had been savaged by war and many buildings had been bombed and burned.

The regiment he was a part of had made a bombed-out building their headquarters by stringing chicken wire across the concrete walls, which was all that remained of the building. This was where they were planning to sleep, eat, and administer their progress. The chicken wire was so the German storm troopers could not throw hand grenades in where they were working or sleeping.

During one night they were attacked by a group of German Storm Troopers that began to throw hand grenades all over the chicken wire cover. Bob heard one grenade find a way through the wire and fall among his 27 comrades. In the dark he grabbed his army blanket and threw it and himself on top of the live grenade.

Of course it exploded, with terrifying damage to Bob, but none of his comrades were even hurt, just scared silly. Their commanding officer called for a retreat and the troops left with the last man out being the commander. He heard Bob groan just as he left and thought he must still be alive. He sent the medics back and Bob's broken body was removed and sent back to England. The war was not over, but for him it was.

I asked Bob what his motivation was for all of this. He explained that he had been raised by his grandparents, logging and making railroad ties in a shop mostly by himself as a teenager. He was bored and bought a little plastic radio to listen to while he worked. The only station he could get was a Christian station.

Bob explained that from hearing all the preaching over his little plastic radio he had come to know about God and he had come to faith in Christ, went to town and was baptized, and decided he could never kill another human.

Not long afterward while still a teenager he had been drafted, but went into the war as a non-combatant. He did carry a pistol, but never shot or killed anyone. He did the most dangerous jobs cheerfully, going ahead of the soldiers, among the enemy, for communication.

Bob was that kind of man, godly, humble, and one of the most unselfish Christians I was ever around. For him he was always just doing his duty. He and Beatrice were busy behind the scenes, busy about the Lord's work.

I noticed that Bob had difficulty walking and asked him what was wrong. He said it was his old war wounds acting up. He explained he had worn out his hips carrying the heavy loads across Africa and Europe.

After further checking I learned both of his hips needed to be replaced, but the military would not do it. His daughter, Linda, and I teamed up and contacted our Senator and soon Bob had surgery and had both of his hips replaced so he could walk without pain again.

Out of hours of discipleship, working in the church, socializing as friends, then traveling together in our RVs, we came to be like loving brothers. He, Beatrice, Margaret, and I spent many hours playing games, eating, and traveling together.

Margaret and I decided to take a cruise to Alaska. We were to catch the ship in Canada. The Maxwells asked if they could go along. We were delighted. Bob had never had a passport, as in the military he did not need one. When he began to try and get one he found that he did not exist. There was no record of his birth or even any evidence of his birth.

After checking everywhere, he learned about his birth and early life. When Bob was born, neither his mother nor father wanted him so they gave him to his maternal grandparents, who raised him as sort of a servant. He found out that his name wasn't even Maxwell and he had a younger brother born later, whom his parents had kept and raised.

His grandparents had a large ranch on the eastern slope of the Rocky Mountains in Colorado. Their business was making railroad ties. When Bob was old enough to work he would take the team of horses and go into the hills, cut down trees, haul them in and hew them into railroad ties, treat them with chemicals, and they would then be sold to the railroad.

Bob told me he usually did this work all alone. He said (as I've already told you) he was lonely and got enough money to buy himself a small radio for $15 so he could listen to music while he worked. He found that there was only one station that came in clearly and it was a Christian station. He said he learned his faith from this source. He learned he needed to be baptized and went to town and found a preacher who baptized him.

After he was out of the war, he studied auto mechanics, specializing in the new electronics on cars. Before long he was teaching this at Lane Community College in Eugene, Oregon, and eventually headed up the department.

When we finally got to go on the Alaskan cruise he still did not have a passport. He was given a letter that proved who he was. We drove to Vancouver, Canada, and caught the cruise ship. We had a glorious couple of weeks on the ship and traveling around in Alaska.

We had traveled to Canada in Bob's new Mercury automobile. His license plate said, "CMH 1 Oregon" At the Canadian/USA border, as we returned home, the guard was a Marine in full white dress uniform. When Bob rolled down the window the guard asked, "What does your license plate mean, CMH 1?" Bob sort of shrugged his shoulders, looking down, sort of embarassed and said nothing. I was in the front passenger seat and leaned over and said to the Marine "Congressional Medal of Honor number one."

The guard immediately snapped to attention, saluted Bob and said, "Welcome home soldier!" He asked if he could have the honor of shaking Bob's hand. He then motioned for us to proceed across the border and home. He did not check any of our passports or Bob's letter telling who he was.

Bob and Beatrice moved to Boise not long after we returned to Idaho so I could be president of Boise Bible College. A few years later, Eagle Christian Church was begun and the preacher, Steve Crane, and Bob Maxwell visited on foot every home in the city of Eagle with a letter of greeting and welcome to the church.

The Maxwells were very helpful members, working hard behind the scenes to build the church. Eagle Christian Church today is what it is in part due to their work behind the scenes.

Many years later Bob died at the age of 94. I was asked to have his funeral. The service was held at the fairgrounds near Redmond, Oregon in a huge arena filled with people, and after the service the roads were lined with people for about twelve miles as we proceeded to the cemetery.

People were standing at attention, cheering and saluting the twelve miles from the arena to the cemetery. This service was broadcast on nationwide television, giving the honor justly due to this Hidden Faith Hero, Robert Dale Maxwell and his lovely wife Beatrice.

Chris Roth

In sixty years of ministry, I do not recall anyone who has worked harder than Chris Roth as a Hidden Faith Hero. When there is a lot of work that is to be done at the church, you will most often find Chris involved.

About 20 years ago she became a member of the local church. Soon afterward she volunteered to prepare the communion.

All ancient churches have weekly communion--Catholic, Greek Orthodox, Syrian Orthodox, or Coptic churches, trace their history back to near the beginning of the church at the Day of Pentecost in A.D. 33. Each of these ancient churches have communion weekly, as this was the practice of the early church.

So New Testament Christian Churches have weekly communion. When Chris began preparing communion, there were just a few hundred people in attendance. As time has passed, this number has grown to several thousand, yet Chris has continued to prepare communion for everyone.

With the coming of Covid-19, a change was made from filling cups to using prefilled cups with bread and juice. These needed to be placed on tables for people to pick up as they entered the lobby for use in the church services. Someone needed to place them on the tables at the many entrances to the large church building. Guess who does this most weeks? Yes, you are right, Chris does. They are perfectly and beautifully spaced and ready for the multiple services. After each service they need to be refurbished, which she does.

I suspect Chris has provided literally millions of cups of communion for Christians. Some Sundays there are many thousands of people in attendance. Recently, for the Christmas Eve services, there were more than 5,000 people in attendance and communion was served.

As soon as she is finished preparing communion, she goes outside one of the east church doors to cheerfully welcome members and guests. Sometimes it is very hot and other times very cold, but Chris is usually there.

If you watch her at church, she is going all around warmly greeting, hugging, and welcoming everyone. She is definitely a not so hidden but a true Faith Hero.

Want to know who the hundreds of Hidden Heroes of the Faith are at your local church? Be at church an hour to one-and-a-half hours early on a Sunday morning and watch the flock of Hidden Heroes coming in to serve the Lord and use their Holy Spirit gifts to minister for our Lord Jesus and His church.

Jerry Baker

Very Few People Are Beyond the Gospel's Redemption, Not Even Jerry Baker

Sometimes I have observed a person's behavior and thought that they were well beyond the help of Jesus and the gospel. They seem to be almost totally evil.

Such was the case with Jerry Baker. His sister-in-law had stopped by the church and greeted me in the parking lot, rolling down the window of her new, big, black Lincoln. She asked to be baptized and was. She told me her husband and brother-in-law operated a nearby golf course and said I could play golf free if I wanted.

A few days later I stopped in and was greeted by Jerry cussing out a person in the most awful and eloquent filthy speech I had ever heard. Even during my years working in a loggers' tire shop had I ever heard so many filthy and irreverent words all strung together.

Jerry Baker, right

When Jerry came up for air, I interrupted him and said, "I take it that you are a man of very high IQ in order to speak so eloquently and profanely." He addressed a few descriptive words at me and asked, "Who the #@%& I was?" I said I was the preacher from the Christian Church and I was looking for the

Baker brothers. He said he was one and his name was Jerry.

A few weeks later I returned and talked to his brother Jim, who was Ruth's husband, the lady I had baptized after the parking lot conversation. Jim had been at the baptism. I had a more calm and decent conversation with the brothers that day and was set up to play golf later that afternoon.

For weeks I sort of made an effort to avoid Jerry, for fear I might get in on one of his hellish cussing episodes.

In a few weeks Jerry's wife, Peggy, and his mother-in-law came and were baptized. I still sort of worked around Jerry, thinking he was beyond reach. But this came to an end when Suzie, Jerry's teenaged daughter, came wanting to be baptized.

I had adopted a policy, several years before, of always talking to the parents before baptizing their children. I approached Jerry and brought up the subject of his daughter's baptism. This unleashed another tirade against Christianity and religion in general. He said it was all just a farce and perpetrated by hypocrites.

I asked him to explain himself and here is what he told me. "I became a Catholic as a teenager and helped with things at church. After high school I decided I wanted to become a Catholic priest. I entered the training and was well on my way when I discovered how immoral and corrupt the priests were. I studied their teachings and found that much was not biblical but corrupt and a distortion of biblical truth. I left the church and promised I would never again have anything to do with such a corrupt system. Thus I am what I am today." (This is not to suggest that all or many Catholics are like the ones Jerry encountered.)

He said he did not want Suzie to get involved in this terrible religion. I did the best to explain to him that Suzie just wanted to turn her life over to Jesus and follow the Lord, whom her Aunt Ruth, mother, and grandmother were following. I was concerned that if he forbade her to follow Jesus she might rebel and get into drugs, pre-marital sex, and ruin her life.

After an hour or two of conversation he finally agreed that if Suzie insisted he would not forbid it, but he would have nothing to do with it himself.

Suzie's baptism was set for the following Sunday evening.

The church building was beautiful with the baptistery up front behind and higher than the pulpit, with beautiful stone work and a huge cross.

The night of the baptism the lights in the baptismal were on, with the church sanctuary darkened. I went into the water first, dressed in a white robe, then Suzie came down the other side, also dressed in white. It was a beautiful scene, almost surreal.

I prepared to say a few words when I saw Jerry sneak into the back of the sanctuary and sit in the dark on the very last row of pews. Due to this, I explained more about baptism than usual and when Suzie came up out of the water I heard someone yelling as he ran down the aisle, "Wait, wait, don't leave the baptistery Charles, I need to give my filthy heart to Jesus also." It was Jerry.

We got Jerry ready and he was soon baptized and he was truly "born again." Jerry was a new man in Christ. This time he was surrounded by godly and loving Christian people.

A few days later Jerry invited me to have lunch with him, so we went down to "Bunch of Lunch" at Shakey's Pizza parlor. We found a quiet place in the corner where we could talk.

Jerry began to give me his history, starting with being an altar boy at the Catholic Church. He enjoyed this service and continued. He decided he wanted to become a Catholic priest and after high school he joined the program and began the long process of training to achieve his goal.

At first things went great, but as he got deeper into the program he was shocked by the hypocrisy, immorality, and corruption. What he found was a program not founded on the Bible, decency, and morality, but of wickedness and sin. The longer he was involved, the more he came to distrust religion and to blame God and Christ for the evil found behind the façade of religion. (As already said, this is not to suggest that all Catholics are like this, but where Jerry was it was corrupt.)

Little by little he became more and more disgusted and finally he left the priesthood training and Catholic Church in failure and deep hurt. He turned from faith in Jesus to evil and hatred of religion in general. This was where I had found him.

At first, understandably, he was suspicious of me and the church in general, but attended regularly and followed the five-point system for the growing and faithful Christian that I had suggested for him:

1. Always attend church, unless sick or impossible for some reason.
2. Never miss the Lord's Supper each weekend.
3. Pray at least five times each day--as you get up in the morning, at meals, and when you go to bed.
4. Faithfully study your Bible.
5. Tithe your money and time.

In a couple of months our going to lunch became quite regular, at least twice a month and then became weekly. During these times we talked about Christianity and the Bible. It became a discipleship relationship and gradually a deep friendship. We began to socialize with him and his wife, Peggy.

He would always insist on paying for our lunches. He was a professional golfer and a good one. He also helped manage the golf course. He made way more money than I did as a preacher. When it came time to pay he would say, "If you have more cash on you than I do then you can pay." He would have a couple of thousand dollars. I never had much except a credit card with a healthy balance due.

In a matter of time I had some stocks that I sold, and I took the $4,000 I got in cash and had it in my wallet. As I recall this was the only time I ever got to pay for lunch. You should have seen him and his brother Jim's eyes when I pulled out all that cash.

We started meeting at an ice cream joint called "Snelgroves" for double-thick, burnt-almond-fudge milkshakes ever so often, in addition to lunches. What began as a cordial minister/member relationship came to be like two blood brothers who loved each deeply.

One day at lunch Jerry told me the sad news that he was moving from Utah to Florida, where he had accepted a job managing a golf course. I was worried about his spiritual future. We kept contact regularly by letter and telephone.

A few weeks after they moved, he told me he was taking Greek at a local Christian college. As mentioned earlier, Jerry's IQ was 170 or almost double normal. He soon mastered Greek. He then took Hebrew and that too soon was mastered. All this time he was studying his Bible faithfully.

He and Peggy were active in a local New Testament church and I learned that he was teaching what was soon to become a rather large Sunday school class. Not much later he told me he was now an Elder in the church, which position he held for many years.

One year we planned our vacation so we could visit the Bakers in Florida. When we arrived Jerry had it set up so we could go together and teach his parents. We taught George and Maude, and Jerry got to baptize his own parents. What a day of rejoicing that was.

After we returned home from vacation, Jerry called to tell me he had taught and baptized his younger brother and family. This meant that the whole Baker family were now Christians.

One year just before Christmas, Jerry and I spent about an hour visiting on the telephone. We had a great time recalling all of the precious events of our lives together. His precious wife, Peggy, had recently died. He told me his brother George had been murdered a few weeks before.

George's youngest son's youngest daughter had just been married and they had traveled out of town to be at the wedding. After the wedding George was hungry and walked to a fast food place near their hotel. As he returned to the hotel three black men attacked him with clubs and beat him to death. When apprehended they said they just wanted to kill a white man.

Jerry and I shed many tears before hanging up. I was sad to learn that Jerry had died in his sleep ten days after our talk. He was 94 years old and now was reunited with his brother, parents and his precious wife, Peggy.

Just think what a great Hidden Hero Jerry Baker was and is. Never think anyone is beyond the reach of the redeeming touch of Lord Jesus. He was and is such a precious friend. I'll be seeing you soon, Faith Hero Jerry.

Fred Becker

When we finally got settled into a permanent parsonage in Salt Lake City, after five moves, a young couple with two small children moved in next door. We were all similar ages and soon struck up a warm friendship that has survived over the years.

Fred Becker was an FBI agent on active duty in Salt Lake City and soon gave me a clearer picture of what was really going on in Salt Lake City behind the scenes in what was supposed to be the new "Paradise in the Mountains."

Mr. & Mrs. Fred Becker

He showed me where the businesses were in Salt Lake City that dealt in stolen merchandise. He showed me that SLC suffered from most of the crimes that afflicted other major cities.

One evening he suggested that I dress up like an FBI agent, in a dark suit, white shirt and dark tie. He would show me what was going on downtown near Temple Square, the Mormon Temple, and near the Mormon worldwide headquarters.

Just two blocks from the Mormon Temple was one of the most active Red Light Districts in America. When we pulled on to Second South and Second West there were 27 ladies of the night practicing their trade.

Fred asked me, "Want to be solicited?" I replied, "Heaven sakes, Fred, NO! I'm a minister of the gospel." So instead he suggested we get out and walk the street a block or two. Reluctantly I agreed, and we were soon greeted by a pretty young lady dressed in a dark blue suit, with bright yellow trim. A fancy car had pulled up and let her out near us.

Fred asked her how much she had earned on that "trick." She said, "Oh, Fred darling," calling him by name, since he worked the "Man Act" and this was one of his responsibilities. She told Fred, "I would never do that for money, I do it for love."

Uneasy, I suggested we move on, which we did.

I begin to follow these events in the local newspaper with more interest since people were often being arrested there, but the judge almost always just threw the cases out of court, saying people had the right to do what they wanted.

Fred asked me one day to go shooting with him. I got my few guns and we went out into the desert where I learned Fred was an "Annie Oakley" shot. I've never seen someone who could shoot and almost never miss. A few years later Fred was transferred to Los Angeles where in FBI competition he shot a perfect 300 score three years in a row.

Well, I'm ahead of the story. The Cranes and Beckers began studying the Bible together and soon they were baptized into Christ and became faithful Christians and even led two other FBI families to Christ who became members of the church.

One day while talking to Fred, he told me he wanted to become a Chief of Police of some major American city. I learned a few years later that he had become the Chief of Police of Grand Junction, Colorado.

Not long after, he called and told me he had been selected as Chief Warden of the Texas State prison system. Since his mother lived in the same city as we did, each year when he came to Idaho to visit her we always had lunch together.

Fred told me he had changed one of the Texas prisons so that anyone who was jailed there had to agree to attend weekly Bible studies. This prison soon became popular because of its very low recidivism numbers. This prison became the model for prisons like it on three continents: America, Europe, and Africa. Fred traveled there to help them set up these prisons programs.

The point of this story is that Fred Becker never was an elder, deacon, Sunday school teacher, singer, nor any other position of public notice, but he helped lead hundreds of people to Christ. People whose lives were broken were led to Christ and to productive lives. Fred Becker, now deceased, deserves the title of Fred Becker, Hidden Faith Hero.

John and Marge Gordon

One thing I observed very early in life was that people in the public eye were frequently the focus of "Groupies" seeking unnatural and sometimes immoral relationships with preachers or people of influence. Being a Christian, I was completely committed to my one and only wife, Margaret, whom I adored.

On the very first Sunday of each ministry I always asked someone else to lead the invitation hymn so Margaret and I could respond to the invitation and publicly place membership with the church to which we would minister.

After being accepted as members, I would give a brief introduction of the family and especially of Margaret, my wife. I would praise her and make it very plain she was my one and only soul mate and wife. This was to make it clear that I was not open to any illicit relationships.

As I concluded these remarks, Margaret, the kids, and I would walk down the aisle together and line up near the exit of the church building. As we walked

down the aisle, side by side, Margaret had a big grin on her face and John and Marge Gordon, sitting near the front, also had big smiles; Margaret winked at John Gordon who winked back. This was the beginning of what turned into a life-long friendship, the young preacher and the much older couple in the church.

At this point we had no idea who or what they were. We were soon to learn what wonderful Christian people the Gordons were. My father was recently deceased and my mother a widow, was far away in Oregon. John and Marge became like parents to us. They became our confidants, counselors, and would visit and encourage us.

The Parsonage

Our home was to be in the church parsonage that was surrounded by the church building on two sides. It had been the parsonage for about 100 years and deferred maintenance was evidenced everywhere. There were pictures of it with horses and buggies lined up all around it when church services were going on nearly 100 years before. The parsonage then looked very much the same as when we moved into it. Everything was run down or broken.

For example, the hot water heater was three/fourths full of lime from the awful city water of this little town. The city water had 11 grains of hardness to each gallon of water.

The plumbing, what there was of it, was shot. The kitchen sink took a half hour to drain. One could not have a hot or warm bath. The one and only toilet was upstairs and the floor was rotted under it so when it was used it would rock back and forth. It was just over the dining room table downstairs.

We often joked that a heavy-set person just might end up on the dining table below on some Sunday after church while we were having lunch. When there was a thunder storm and heavy rain, the electricity would go off and the basement would get a couple of feet of water in it. The gas water heater, washer, and dryer were on two concrete blocks, set on top of each other, so the appliances would not be ruined by flooding water.

The elders decided it was time to build a new parsonage. Since the church was doing so well and the offerings so generous, there was money to build one. Most of this story will remain untold at this time, but just the parts that show what wonderful people the Gordons were will be the focus now.

When the house was to be torn down, we had to find a place to live. There was not one house in town or nearby that was vacant where we could move. In the midst of this search a young couple, not members of the church, came forward saying they had a small house that was about three/fourths finished, and that if we would complete some plumbing and wiring they would rent it to the church.

Being somewhat handy, I partially finished connecting the plumbing under the house and finished the wiring. There had been heavy rains and I crawled around in water and mud to do this work. I never did have time to connect the washer and dryer. My work passed inspection, with a few modifications, and the five of us moved into about 900 square feet, a very small two-bedroom bungalow.

Since the house was so small, about half of our possessions were put into a classroom at the church. We just got moved in when Margaret got a phone call from her father, George, asking for her to come home to help since her mother was dying with brain cancer. While I was in Seminary and ministering to the large church, I was alone with the children and I was a full-time Seminary student as well.

I would be at the laundromat at midnight doing our clothing, washing, drying, and folding.

In the midst of all this, one Thursday evening a man came to the door of the small house and said in a disgusted voice, "What are you doing living in my house? I'm moving in here tomorrow!" The young, non-Christian couple had a chance to sell the house for cash and cared little about truth or decency, so had not told the new owner it was rented and occupied.

This threw me into a panic.

I called the church prayer team and the message went out throughout the church membership on the prayer chain. In less than an hour John Gordon showed up at the door and said his father's old mansion was empty and thoroughly furnished and we could move in that evening. His father had recently died and it was empty. He and I gathered a crew of people, men and woman and the rest of our things were put in the church Sunday school classroom, filling it to the ceiling and door.

We went from a small awful place to a big mansion. Even the bed I was to sleep in had a canopy over it. It was a glorious place with every modern convenience. The house had lots of room, many bedrooms, big garage, barn, and big yard for the boys to mow.

There was a cattle water tank by the barn, and the boys fished in Flat Branch creek and brought live fish and put them in the cattle water tank.

When Margaret returned from her three-and-one-half months of caring for her dying mother, she had no idea where anything was—clothes, dishes, washer, dryer, etc. Carol Beth soon had her mother oriented. It was not hard to get used to this beautiful old mansion with all the modern conveniences.

During this move Margaret was with her mother. We had just got sort of settled when Margaret called from Coos Bay, Oregon to say her mother had died and she hoped we could all come to the funeral. It seemed totally financially impossible. I still hadn't paid for her plane ticket out to care for her mother, it was on a credit card. I prayed later that evening, on my knees, for God to give me wisdom to know how to proceed.

In the morning John Gordon came to the house and asked if he could come in and visit with me. We sat at the kitchen table and he pulled out a check that was dated and signed but the amount was blank.

John said, "Marge and I want your whole family to go to the funeral. Fill in the amount you need to cover all your travel expenses."

I looked at it as tears ran down my face and said to John, "How much should I write it for?" He said, "Would $25,000 be enough?"

I replied, "Oh that is way too much John, but $5,000 would be more than adequate." He took the check and filled it out for $5,000 and gave it to back to me.

This paid for Margaret's plane ticket and for the rest of us to travel to Coos Bay, Oregon, for Joyce Almira Colver Ross's funeral and back home again to Illinois. While out west we traveled on to California where I had been invited to speak at the North American Christian Convention. We came home from the memorial service debt free because of the generosity of John and Marge Gordon.

In a couple of months the new parsonage was ready and we could finally settle into our own home with our own things. The new house was superb. It even had a drain in the over-large double garage so one could wash their cars inside the garage in the winter months.

The new house had a great water heater for hot baths. There was a backup battery for the sump pump so the basement no longer flooded during a storm when there was no electricity.

And if I needed a kind ear to talk to, John and Marge were always there. What wonderful Hidden Faith Heroes they were in this small Midwestern town of Moweaqua, Illinois. Most churches would be blessed if they had a family or two like the Gordons, Hidden Faith Heroes.

An Unnamed Man

A member of this man's family thought the story should be told, but his name not given, as some of the family may not be familiar with the details as best I recall them.

At Sunday morning church, this man's parents asked if I would call on him and his wife that week. I did as I had promised, and showed up at their house out on the farm. His wife welcomed me into the house.

In came Ivan (not his real name) who was huge, 6 foot 7 inches and weighing about 275 lbs. He asked, "Did my folks ask you to come try to get me to take the bath?" He then asked me to sit down and he would be right back. He went into the kitchen and returned with two cans of beer, one of which he threw to me.

I said to Ivan that I did not drink beer. He said to me, "If I take the bath I suppose I will have to quit my beer and cigarettes?" I replied, "Ivan, if I sat here all afternoon and told you all the things that the Lord will change in your life I might not get through, but I promise He won't change anything that doesn't need to be changed."

He said, "You are rather blunt, aren't you?" I said, "Just like you."

This led into a discussion of why he needed to be the spiritual leader of his wife and children. We had a good Bible study and we met again the next week and I went over The Roman Road to Salvation with him and his wife, Carla. That afternoon I baptized Ivan and his wife.

They began attending church regularly and soon we bonded as warm friends and remain so to this day. He wanted to get involved in some form of ministry and I suggested that he become a part of Bold Ones, an evangelistic outreach group that I discipled, and then they called on prospective members and the unsaved.

We met each Tuesday evening at 6:30 for Kentucky Fried Chicken, which they ate, while I gave them a lesson on evangelism and discipleship. After the lesson, cards were handed out for each team of two to visit people in their homes.

Ivan was soon excelling in this work; his direct manner and recent conversion left him excited about the changes in his and his wife's lives.

One man that I had been calling on for several months, with little apparent success, I decided to send Ivan to visit. That very evening he brought him back to be baptized, which Ivan did.

The man later said, "You sent this giant out to call on me and I found it impossible to resist his urging to accept Christ and be the spiritual leader in my home."

Within six months Ivan became a Sunday school teacher of the junior high boy's class. I felt this was a bit soon, remembering Ivan's past, but the Sunday school superintendent was sure he was ready.

Ivan had been a basketball and baseball star in high school and college. He had earned his degree to teach high school, and had taught for several years before returning to the family farm where he was needed.

In the first quarter year, or thirteen weeks, 49 people were baptized. I had only taught one of them; the rest were all brought by the Bold Ones, but especially the junior high boys from Ivan's class, which was the largest group of the 49 who were baptized.

It was no great shock when Ivan came to me a few months later and said he had decided to become a preacher of the gospel and wanted to enroll in Bible college to get a second degree in preaching, which he did.

Not long after his graduation, Ivan was off to seminary to earn a couple of advanced degrees in ministry. Today Ivan is preaching at a church and using his skills as a soul winner—a true Faith Hero, no longer hidden.

The message is clear that God has gifted all Christians with skills or gifts of the Holy Spirit to serve the Kingdom. Hidden Heroes often become very visible Faith Heroes.

I thank God for my dearly loved friend Ivan and all the people who will be in Heaven because he gave his heart and life to Jesus at first as a Hidden Faith Hero.

All Heroes of the Faith, Hidden or Public, Are Gifted by the Holy Spirit

All Heroes of the Faith, whether public or secret, have a glorious future. Each of us needs to use the gifts given to us by the Holy Spirit at our conversion, whether it be some glorious public gift, or something not seen by mankind, but known only to our Lord, we all have a chance to serve and a glorious reward for service when we get to Heaven.

Acts 2:38–39 makes it clear that all Christians have the Holy Spirit:

> "And Peter said to them, "Repent and be baptized every one of you in the name of Jesus Christ for the forgiveness of your sins and you will receive the gift of the Holy Spirit … For the promise is for you and … for all that are far off, everyone…"

> "But the fruit of the Spirit is love, joy, peace, patience, kindness, goodness, faithfulness, gentleness, self-control; against such things there is no law. And those who belong to Christ Jesus have crucified the flesh with its passions and desires" (Galatians 5:22–24).

> "But grace was given to each one of us according to the measure of Christ's gift. Therefore it says, 'When he ascended on high he led a host of captives, and he gave gifts to men.'…And he gave the Apostles, the prophets, the evangelists, the shepherds and teachers, to equip the saints

for the work of ministry, for the building up the body of Christ, until we all attain to the unity of the faith and the knowledge of the Son God, to mature manhood, to the measure of the stature of the fullness of Christ.

This seems to indicate that all Christians are gifted to be public or Hidden Faith Heroes. This means all God's children have been given some talent or ability that is needed in the kingdom or church.

One writer suggests that the New Testament lists over fifty gifts of the Holy Spirit that may be given to the Christian.

Here is a partial list:

Romans 12:6—

- Prophecy
- Serving
- Teaching
- Exhorting
- Contributing
- Leading
- Loving
- Showing honor
- Affection
- Zeal
- Hospitality
- Feeding enemies

I Corinthians 12:4—

- Wisdom
- Knowledge
- Faith
- Miracles
- Prophecy, "forth-telling, not just foretelling"
- Tongues
- Interpretation of tongues

Apostles
Helping
Administration

I Corinthians 13—

Faith
Hope
Love is the foremost gift of all (I Corinthians 13:13)

Ephesians 4:7—

Evangelists
Shepherds
Teachers
Ministry

The above lists have thirty gifts of the Spirit and many more could be added. Anything that furthers the work of the church of Christ can be fed and nurtured by the Holy Spirit for Christ's work on earth.

Each of us needs to seek to discover how the Spirit has gifted us to serve the church and others. At the center of this service is love of Christ and our Christian brothers and sisters. If it is not of love it is not Holy Spirit driven.

If a person is cantankerous and difficult to get along with, fault finding and a trouble maker, dividing the body of Christ, they may be spirit filled, but not the Spirit of Christ, but of Satan.

When we all get to work using our Holy Spirit given gifts, the church cannot help but flourish and spread across our communities, nation, and world.

What is your gift, and are you using it to build up others and the body of Christ? Often the church has neglected to place the emphasis on this truth that it deserves. What is your gift or gifts?

Seek your gift in prayer and meditation and then look for a place to put it, or them, to use. You will be a Faith Hero.

The Future of Spirit-Filled Christians

Heaven

In a time of meditation and prayer about the stories in this book, my mind turned to the future that all the saved have before them. It reminded me of what a preacher said in a sermon that I heard when a teenager.

He said eternity was so long that if a little sparrow bird came once every one thousand years to sharpen its beak on the Rock of Gibraltar, that when this huge rock was worn down to the size of a marble that would only be the first day of Heaven.

A billion years is just a tiny beginning on our future with Jesus. To think of the promised rewards to us servants of God, whether public or private, is to realize just how wonderful our Lord and Savior Jesus really is. That such a gift has been given to us speaks of God's grace. Why would any thinking person reject this gift of salvation?

Yes, we do suffer some, or sometimes much, as Christians. Yes, we give of ourselves in service public and private. But God rewards us so bountifully our minds are unable to comprehend it.

> "Eye has not seen, nor ear heard, or has it entered into the mind of man what God has laid up for those who serve Him." "For God so loved the world that He gave His only begotten Son that whosoever believeth in Him shall not perish but have everlasting life" (John 3:16).

Heaven Has:

Heaven will be a glorious place, with many of the things we love most about this present earth. Here is a partial list taken just from three chapters of the Bible:

John 14:1–2

> Many mansions

Revelation 21—22

> Cities
> Gates
> Streets
> Rivers
> Trees
> Fruits
> Precious stones
> Gold
> Pearls
> Animals
> Singing—worship
> Light
> No oceans
> No tears
> Everything is new
> Spring of the water of life
> Nothing unclean
> Rewards for service
> Lots of people, saints

And the list could go on and on. Just imagine what He has had time to create, with what he did in six days in the original creation. Most of all, there will be no sickness, death, sin, evil, drunkenness, divorce, fatherless children, face masks, shots in the arm ... all will be made new and perfect. I'm ready to go, when He calls. Why should any of us fear death?

<u>Those Who Reject Christ</u>

On the other hand, what is the future of those who, due to their selfishness and godlessness, reject Jesus, living selfish lives of sin, destruction of themselves and the ruin of other people? Unfortunately for them their eternity is the same length as heaven.

> "Then he will say to those on his left, 'Depart from me, you cursed, into the eternal fire prepared for the devil and his angels, For I was hungry and you gave me no food, I was thirsty and you gave me no drink, I was a stranger and you did not welcome me, naked and you did not clothe me, sick and in prison and you did not visit me,' Then they also will answer, saying, 'Lord, when did we see you hungry or thirsty or a stranger or naked or sick or in prison, and did not minister to you?' Then he will answer them, saying, 'Truly, I say to you, as you did not do it to one of the least of these, you did not do it to me' and these will go away into eternal punishment, but the righteous into eternal life" (Matthew 25:41-46).

These words are given by Jesus Himself. He makes it clear that the duration of Heaven and Hell are the same length—eternal. Those who have accepted Christ as Savior and Lord and lived lives of kindness and service to Him and others will go to heaven. Those who have lived selfish lives of sin and unbelief will go to Hell for eternity.

The very thought is frightening! Imagine dying and entering into Hell forever and ever. The Greek word in Matthew 25:46 is (*aonia*) forever and forever. It is the same word that tells us how long Heaven will be. There are no EXIT signs from Hell.

The first day of Hell is the same length as the first day of Heaven. The sparrow sharpening its beak on the Rock of Gibraltar once every one thousand years and finally wearing it down to the size of a marble is but the first day. There are no EXIT signs.

The enormity and disaster of ending in Hell is so awful and gruesome that you must please be warned, accept Jesus now. Life is short—don't waste it serving the Devil. Serving the Devil is a life of selfishness, waste, disaster, destruction and awful unhappiness in life and unimaginable awful recompense in Hell.

Biblical Descriptions of Hell

Matthew 25:46 "eternal punishment"
Philippians 3:19 "end is destruction"
II Thessalonians 1:9 "punishment of eternal destruction"
Hebrews 10:39 "destroyed"
II Peter 2:17 "the doom of utter darkness"
Jude 13 "gloom of utter darkness"
Revelation 2:13 "where Satan dwells"
  19:20 "thrown into the lake of fire that burns with sulphur"
  20:6 "Second death" (Greek Thanatos, "loss of well-being, not loss of being")
  21:8 "their place will be in the lake of fire"
  20:10 "thrown into the lake of fire and sulphur…where they will be tormented day and night forever and ever."

These are but a few of the awful descriptions of Hell. It talks of worms, pain, hopelessness, without end, and just as long as Heaven.

Why would God do such a thing to any human? He doesn't! God has called them all their lives by the book of nature with all its evidences of Him. Gospel music has called, preaching called, the Bible called, missionaries, Grace, Faith, Love has called, evangelism repeatedly invited them and instead they had rejected

Him and all His calls to free salvation, walking past the church, the Cross of Christ, Christmas, Easter, their grandmother's and grandfather's prayers, literally walking through the blood of Christ at the foot of His Cross and selfishly serving pleasure, sin, lust, anger, killing, they have refused to be worthwhile, loving, helping the poor and sick. Every effort of Jesus to call them has been rejected in their intellectual pride they finally pass into eternity to their eternal ghastly future that they have chosen. God has not done this to them, they have insisted on going there.

In the New Testament, Hell is most often warned about by Jesus Himself. He uses the most awful events possible to picture it. He speaks of outer darkness, the lake of fire, where the fire is never quenched, to be tormented day and night forever and ever, where the Devil and all his angels are one's companions forever.

The first ten minutes of Hell must seem like an eternity. Just imagine being in torment forever and ever with no hope of ever going free. How could any human be so stupid as to reject Jesus' offer of free salvation, through faith, repentance, and baptism? At least we should take time to investigate it thoroughly.

Jesus invites us all, "Come unto me all of you that labor and are heavy laden and I will give you rest." "God is not willing that any should perish but all come to repentance." But you have the right, as a free moral agent, to say yes or no. Accept Him now. Today is the day of salvation!

I beg of you—please accept His free salvation, what do you have to lose? Everything! There are no EXIT signs in Heaven or Hell. Experience the good life as a happy Christian on earth and spend eternity with those you love.

Epilogue

If you have read this far, you may be interested in a bit of background about the churches mentioned and why we transitioned from one to another and how God has had His hand in our lives.

As a young minister in Sutherlin, Oregon, I felt God had been overly generous in giving me a place to minister. I loved every member of the church and had no dream of anything more for my life.

After three-and-a-half years, one member of the church decided it was time for us to move on. (He may have been thinking of the Denominational practice of the preacher moving every two years.) He confronted me in person. I was horrified and had no wish to go anywhere else. I believed that the rest of the membership supported my continuing on as their preacher.

At the same time, a minister in a nearby church said he believed God had been preparing us for our next ministry in Salt Lake City, Utah. He pointed out that from the time I was 13, my whole life had prepared us for the Utah challenge.

He gave me the names of Robert and Toni Thomas and suggested that I call them, which I did. They had been transferred from Colorado to Utah by Bob's job. Since there was no New Testament church anywhere near where they lived, they began having Bible studies in their large basement family room.

Erskine Scates and Earl Heald, from Intermountain Bible College in Grand Junction, Colorado, came to help them begin. Out of this Bible study the new church had begun. They had not yet had a full-time preacher and were seeking one.

I called Bob and he urged me to come try out for the job. I rode the Greyhound Bus from Roseburg, Oregon, to their home in SLC. I preached and was hired. The church at that time was more of an idea than a reality as there were only 42 (sort of) members.

Toni and Bob Thomas

But through prayer and lots of hard work the church began to grow after we came. After the first year of our ministry, one day Dr. Edwin Hayden, Editor of the *Christian Standard* magazine, was coming to town and called to ask if he could speak at the new church. Somehow he had heard about this mission project and wanted to check it out.

We advertised his coming and the Sunday he preached, the church was packed to hear Dr. Hayden. When the invitation hymn was sung, eleven people responded to the invitation to accept Christ and be baptized. All of them were Mormons.

They had been taught and would have responded whoever was preaching, but Dr. Hayden gave a great sermon and was impressed by the baptisms and after church asked if he could take a few pictures, which he did. Shown here and on the next page are two of those pictures, the inside and outside of the church building.

A few weeks later

the lead story in the *Christian Standard* magazine was about Southeast Christian Church, with these two pictures. Almost immediately the church became the focus of national attention and the little-known preacher became known all over the USA and beyond.

The invitations to speak began to pour in, from the North American Christian Convention, the National Missionary Convention, colleges, and churches across half of America and beyond. It became apparent that the Lord had brought us to Utah with this in mind, as LDS people everywhere began to see the light and accept the real Jesus.

This led to my being in one of the most popular religious movies in that ten-year period, *The God-makers*. An estimated one quarter million LDS people came to Christ from these false prophets and this unscriptural religion.

When moving to Salt Lake City, in the back of my mind was the possibility of further theological education. After arrival I was disappointed to learn there was no further theological education available in Utah. I participated in classes offered by Johnson Christian University and Emanuel Christian Seminary.

Even though the church had grown and was strong, the constant opposition of the LDS church and lack of Christian fellowship, with like-minded brethren, began to take its toll. The church was under opposition every day due to the large number of LDS becoming Christians.

In visiting with Dr. Wayne Shaw, at a North

American Christian Convention, he suggested that it was time to pursue my educational dreams by enrolling in Lincoln Christian Seminary. Dr. Shaw told me that when we would leave SLC and drive East over the Wasatch Mountains, heading to Illinois, I would feel like a saddle was taken off my back and the spurs pulled out of my ribs.

One of the main issues was the several high-up leaders and influential Mormons who had come to Christ, including a son of the then current Prophet and grandchildren of one of the LDS Apostles. Several other well-known Mormons being baptized had drawn the attention of the main LDS leadership. Threats were even made against my life and efforts to hurt me were tried.

But the main reason for moving on was for the good of my wife and children, who were being damaged by the constant pressure against their husband and father.

The Move to Illinois

Five churches in the Midwest, looking for a preacher, were suggested to us. We chose the most likely one that was closest to Lincoln Christian Seminary. We came to be interviewed by Moweaqua Christian Church, in the small town called Moweaqua.

I met with the elders on a week night and after being interview for a couple of hours, they voted to hire me. I asked, "Doesn't the church have to vote also?" The elders said, "We know our flock and if they don't love you we will be shocked. Go use our phone to call the other four churches and tell them you have been hired."

There was a large number of people that voted and only one nay vote among them. Two people told me they had cast that vote because they wanted to keep me humble. Probably it was neither.

This wonderful and biblical church was a blessing to our family the whole time of our ministry there. The population sign on the highway coming from the north said the population was 1,500. The one on the same road from the south said 1,400.

The church had over 800 members. The high school principal was a deacon and the grade school principal was an elder in the church. Three of the five school board members were members of the church as were nearly half of the teachers. It was a nearly a perfect place to raise children as anyplace anywhere. It was a wonderful town and even better church, the finest I've known in my life.

Seminary and Caldwell, Idaho

Transitioning from SLC to Seminary was like traveling from a foreign country to paradise. The loving community at Lincoln Christian College and Seminary was filled with glorious champions of the Faith. The classes were all top quality and inspirational. Margaret and I soon healed up. We loved it there. Living in Moweaqua was wonderful.

Illinois at that time had over 600 Christian churches and did not need our long-term ministry, but the West did. I explained to the elders in Moweaqua that my plan was to stay three years and we did.

The second year at the Seminary I was asked to teach, which I did the final two years. Adding teaching to being a full-time student and preacher of a good-sized church meant our lives were super busy. Margaret was also a full-time student and mother of three. But all together our family was very blessed by our time in down state Illinois,

When finished with the desired degrees and both of us had completed our courses, a church in Caldwell, Idaho, sought our help. We loved the Moweaqua church, but knew our goal was to evangelize the West, so we accepted the call to Idaho. We began our ministry there July 1, 1976.

The elders agreed that I could continue and complete my doctoral work and degree. They even supplied a full-time secretary to assist in this massive task. On May 5, 1978, I officially became Dr. Charles A. Crane. The five-and-one-half years of constant work were completed.

The Caldwell church grew during this whole time and ended up with a membership of 1,183. The problem was the church facility was entirely too small for the crowds of people attending. We had multiple church services and classes everywhere. Parking was at a premium and guests could not find a place to park.

Church leadership voted to find a new location, and 17 acres in the most prime address in town was found and purchased. It was soon paid for by generous members.

Plans were made for the much-needed new facility. It would have seated more than twice what the old one did. There would be lots of great classrooms. A standard-sized gym, with kitchen was planned. Near the entrance to the main Sanctuary was a planned high rise-retirement facility with 125 apartments. The residents could ride the elevator and come out near the main entrance to the church building. The US government would fund the retirement home and in twenty-five years it would become the property of the church.

When this plan was presented to the twelve elders, five said yes and seven said no. One elder said, "We built and paid for our church building. Let all these new people build and pay for their own buildings. Why should we have to pay for a church for them?" I was heart sick, realizing that some of the elders may not even be Christians. Later I learned a couple of the vocal ones weren't.

Santa Clara Church of Christ
Eugene, Oregon

What the seven elders did not know was that a church in Eugene, Oregon, had been trying to hire me as their preacher. I was getting a long distance phone call every Monday morning from an elder, Ken Hodney, from Santa Clara Church of Christ in Eugene.

The Eugene church had suffered a couple of devastating problems in quick succession. A couple of influential members had become involved in un-Christian behavior that had split the church.

In the midst of this crisis, a neighborhood boy decided he wanted to burn the church building down. At 2 A.M. Monday morning, he broke into the building with five gallons of gasoline. He poured a trail clear through the building and before exiting he threw a match, and the building was totally engulfed in flames.

Within three hundred yards of the church building was the local fire station. No one was told of the fire and the firemen slept through the whole thing. The beautiful church burned totally down. Everything was destroyed—the pianos, organs, and even the offering and communion trays were melted into ingots.

Recently the church fire insurance had been increased from $400,000 to $900,000. by the trustees. The only problem was the insurance agent had neglected to have the increase reported to the insurance company. The church had to spend $40,000 in attorney fees to get the $400,000. that was due them. This amount would not even frame in a new building.

By faith the church proceeded to build anyway, but when the money was all gone the new building only had a roof, walls, but not even doors or windows. It was short of completion by more than a million dollars.

The congregation had been split by the leadership's sins and only about 62 members remained of what had once been a strong church. The church was headed for closure.

Ken kept calling me and saying, "Come be our preacher, or find us a preacher, if you don't this church will close and it will be your fault."

My mother lived about 45 miles away from this church and while visiting her from Idaho I decided to go see this mess. I was shown around the beginning of the new building by an elder, Archie Powell, whose faith in what they had begun was like a shining light. I was impressed.

The new building was a somewhat smaller edition of what I had planned for Caldwell Christian Church in Idaho. It would seat about 750, had lots of classrooms, a chapel, gym, library, wonderful planned kitchen and lots of parking. The office building was separate from the church building and had not burned.

I asked Archie how much money they had left to complete the building and he said it had all been spent. They had applied for a loan with David Pace from Intermountain Church Planters in Denver, Colorado. They were awaiting a reply as to whether they would get the loan or not.

I returned home to Idaho to learn that the church expansion plans in Caldwell were dead. Of course Ken Hodney called me each Monday, stressing that the future of Santa Clara Church of Christ was now in my hands. The next move was mine. Ken's calls were always loving and polite.

That Sunday a group of people from Eugene showed up in Caldwell and filled two whole pews. Several expressed their opinion that I needed to accept their invitation to become their preacher.

In the middle of the week I received a call from David Pace from the church loaning agency in Denver. David and I had been friends several years. David told me that the loan to the Eugene church would only be approved if I became their preacher, otherwise they would be told no.

I was perplexed that Archie Powell seemed to have more commitment to evangelism and faith to build than all 12 elders in Idaho. Idaho had 1,182 members and Eugene had 62. From research I had learned that Eugene was one of the least evangelized major cities in America, with more than 300,000 people within a 30-minute drive of the church. Only 10% of the community ever went to church.

After a lot of prayer and a few more calls from Ken Hodney, it appeared that God wanted me in Eugene, and Margaret and I accepted the call come work with them. The church was meeting in an Assembly of God church building as they had no building, only a beginning structure.

Margaret needed surgery and remained in Caldwell and I moved to Eugene in my pickup with a camper on it. I parked next to the office complex. I used the bathroom facilities in the church office.

One morning I had neglected to call Sonatrol to tell them I was in the office, when I went in to bathe. I was showering when the shower door opened and there stood an officer with his gun pointed at me. He said, "Please identify yourself!" I replied, "As you can see I have no identification on me." We laughed and I dried, dressed, and showed him my identification. After that I always called the security system when I entered the office.

With the loan from Denver, we proceeded to finish the sanctuary, baptistery, and lobby. In a few weeks we were installing the pews and using the baptistery regularly. In just 17 weeks 77 new members were added. The first person baptized in the new sanctuary was Darrel Phillips. He became a lifelong friend with his wife Betty.

The church grew and we completed the classroom wing, gym, kitchen, library, chapel, and parking lots. It was a wonderful facility. We had ice cream socials and the donated money bought song books. A doctor from Texas, son-in-law of Al and Elsie Tiffen, bought a beautiful grand piano for the church.

Margaret and I agreed to donate all fees we received from funerals and revivals to an organ fund. We had huge garage sales and soon had the money to buy a great church organ. The services were filled with glorious music of every kind.

The church soon grew to be a strong and stable church of Christ, with people from all over Lane County attending.

Boise Bible College

When the Santa Clara Church building was finished and I could begin to breathe more easily, Boise Bible College began to seek me to become their President. It was the last thing I wanted to do. Three other Bible colleges had tried to hire me. My love and heart was in the church and ministry.

I was invited to have lunch with Boise Bible College's Board Chairman Bruce Wheeler. We were to meet in Sisters. When I got there, the President, Academic Dean, and Bruce showed up. They tried to convince me to accept the job. I told them we wanted to stay where we were.

A couple of months later I received an invitation to speak for chapel at the college. When I arrived, I was scheduled not only to speak in chapel but to meet with the President, Dean, and the College Board of Directors.

While talking with the Academic Dean, someone knocked on the door and asked to come in. It was Kenneth Beckman. He entered and got down on one knee in front of my chair and began to tap me on the chest and saying, "We have checked all over America and prayed earnestly, and you are to be the next President of Boise Bible College. If you do not do this you are just like Jonah, running from God's will for your life." He then got up, excused himself and left.

After he left, Margaret looked at me and said, "Well, Jonah, what are you going to do?"

Later that evening we learned there was a banquet planned at a local restaurant with the entire College Board. When we arrived and had eaten our meal, the Board Chairman again offered me the job and asked that we go into an adjoining room, and when we had decided to give them a yes answer we were then to return and accept the job.

Margaret and I went into the next room and prayerfully talked it over and decided that even though neither of us wanted to do this, it appeared to be of God's leading. We returned to accept the offer of the job. From the beginning, it was the last on my list of goals for my life.

I returned to Eugene with a heavy heart. We had just gotten to a place where I could focus on evangelism, leaving building and fund raising behind, and here I was faced with another nearly impossible task.

Boise Bible College's campus had been described as a "run-down Motel 6 in a cow pasture." Deferred maintenance was everywhere. The dorms were run down. The dorm bedrooms served as classrooms. The chapel was in two bedrooms with the wall between taken out. The library was in the corner of the gym, the grounds were covered with sagebrush and tons of large rocks, and the front half of the campus was broken-down barbed wire fences, horse biscuits, goat heads, and sagebrush. It looked totally neglected.

The finances were a disaster—there was a first, second, and third mortgage on the campus. The line of credit at the bank had not even had the interest paid on it in over two years. There was a big stack of notes, due and payable, in the college safe. The interest due on the notes was 10% and were on notes from $5,000 to $25,000. Some notes were five or more years old. Income did not even meet current expenses, let alone begin to retire the debt.

My doctorate had four majors: Communication, Administration, Spiritual Development, and Writing. One of my first tasks was to make a 25-year plan for BBC. Goals were set and how to reach these goals was planned.

A whole new campus was planned, built, and paid for. There was the new office building, library, rare book room, computer center, classrooms, small chapel, large classrooms, large chapel, and dorms. A large maintenance shop was built. The old buildings were repaired and modernized. A fine sports field with baseball and football fields was completed. All of the mess that had been there was replaced with beautiful landscaping and trees.

Finally, after 18.5 years, at age 69, I retired. This was due in large part to having been hit head on by a drunk driver on Highway 44 near Middleton, Idaho. This required seven surgeries.

Since retirement I have given my life and influence to help build Eagle Christian Church. Why consider this Epilogue? It appears that since accepting Christ and being baptized at age 13, God has had His hand on my life. I'm suggesting that if you look closely at your life you will observe that when you turn your life over to Him He will guide and direct you. What may look like a disaster may be God redirecting you to what He has next for you to do with your spiritual gifts.

All Christians are gifted for ministry for Christ in hundreds of different ways. What are your gifts? Discover them, then use them to His glory.

Other Books by Dr. Charles A. Crane

1. *Do You Know What the Mormon Church Teaches?*
   (A brief comparison of Bible teaching and Mormon Doctrine)
2. *Mormon Missionaries in Flight*
   (Why a Mormon Missionary does not want to talk to a knowledgeable Christian)
3. *The Bible and Mormon Scriptures Compared*
   (A Text Critical comparison of the Bible and Mormon Scriptures)
4. *Ashamed of Joseph*
   (An accurate biography of Joseph Smith)
5. *Christianity and Mormonism, from Bondage to Freedom*
   (Christ brings freedom from Mormon bondage)
6. *Is Mormonism Christian?*
   (This is a rewrite of Harry Ropp's fine book after his untimely death.)
7. *Autobiography of Charles A. Crane*
8. *A Practical Guide to Soul Winning* (Discipleship)
   (Biblical management of the church for evangelism and growth)
9. *Personal Family Finance*
   (Becoming affluent with modest income)

10. *The Bible—The True and Reliable Word of God*
    (The result of fifty years of study of ancient Biblical manuscripts)
11. *The Families of Man Archaeologically and Biblically Traced* (Humanity today can be traced back to Noah and the Ark)
12. *The Adventures of a Young Preacher*
    (A fun book showing the value of preachers, even young ones)
13. *Adventures of a Young Preacher in Salt Lake City*
    (Volume 2 in the Young Preacher series)
14. *The Young Preacher Goes to Seminary*
    (Volume 3 in the Young Preacher series)
15. *Irrefutable Proof that Jesus Is the Messiah.*
    (Three things that are positive proof we have a Savior)

www.ingramcontent.com/pod-product-compliance
Lightning Source LLC
LaVergne TN
LVHW051526070426
835507LV00023B/3322